To C

with lo

Cousin Margaret Love
+ family

September 21 / 2015
Grande Prairie B.

ÉTIENNE BRÛLÉ

AMAZING STORIES

ÉTIENNE BRÛLÉ

The Mysterious Life and Times
of an Early Canadian Legend

HISTORY/BIOGRAPHY
by Gail Douglas

To Tom

PUBLISHED BY ALTITUDE PUBLISHING CANADA LTD.
1500 Railway Avenue, Canmore, Alberta T1W 1P6
www.altitudepublishing.com
1-800-957-6888

Publisher	Stephen Hutchings
Associate Publisher	Kara Turner
Editor	Gayl Veinotte
Digital art colouring & maps	Scott Manktelow

We acknowledge the financial support of the Government
of Canada through the Book Publishing Industry Development
Program (BPIDP) for our publishing activities.

Altitude GreenTree Program
Altitude Publishing will plant twice as many trees as were used
in the manufacturing of this product.

National Library of Canada Cataloguing in Publication Data

Douglas, Gail
Étienne Brûlé / Gail Douglas.

(Amazing stories)
Includes bibliographical references.
ISBN 1-55153-961-6

1. Brûlé, Étienne, 1591?-1632. 2. Canada--Discovery and exploration--French.
3. Canada--History--To 1663 (New France). 4. Coureurs de bois--Canada--
Biography. I. Title. II. Series: Amazing stories (Canmore, Alta.)

FC332.1.B7D68 2003   971.01'13'092   C2003-905481-0

An application for the trademark for Amazing Stories™
has been made and the registered trademark is pending.

Printed and bound in Canada by Friesens
2 4 6 8 9 7 5 3 1

Cover: Samuel de Champlain and possibly
Étienne Brûlé depicted at an Iroquois council fire

Contents

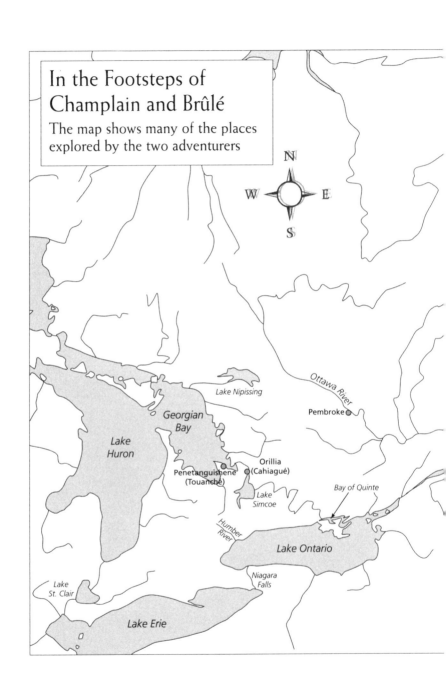

In the Footsteps of Champlain and Brûlé

The map shows many of the places explored by the two adventurers

N
W E
S

Lake Nipissing

Ottawa River

Pembroke

Georgian Bay

Lake Huron

Orillia (Cahiagué)

Penetanguishene (Touanché)

Lake Simcoe

Bay of Quinte

Humber River

Lake Ontario

Lake St. Clair

Niagara Falls

Lake Erie

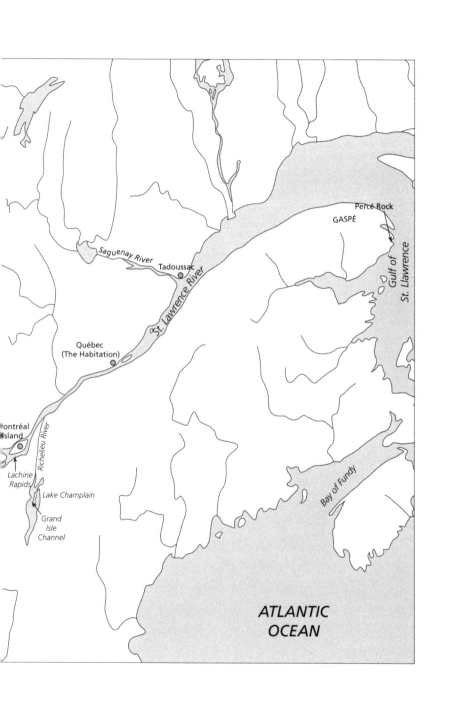

Percé Rock

GASPÉ

Gulf of
St. Lawrence

Saguenay River

Tadoussac

St. Lawrence River

Québec
(The Habitation)

Montréal
Island

Richelieu River

Lachine
Rapids

Lake Champlain

Grand
Isle
Channel

Bay of Fundy

ATLANTIC
OCEAN

Prologue

So this is how it would end. Tied to a torture post, suffering unspeakable torments, utterly hopeless.

It was bad luck that he had become separated from his Huron guides and lost in the forest, but stupid for him to have thrown himself at the mercy of the Iroquois.

"Are you not one of those Frenchmen?" they asked him. "Those men of iron who make war on us?"

He denied it, shamelessly lying in a desperate bid to save himself. "I am from a nation much better than the French," he said, "and I am a good friend of the Iroquois."

Did he really think they would believe him?

He only hoped he could show courage right to the end. Courage, indifference, defiance. It was all he had left. He thought back to the Iroquois prisoners he had seen captured by his Huron friends after a skirmish. No matter how they suffered, they refused to show despair. Would he be able to do as much?

His eyes were stinging and his vision was cloudy, but he saw one of the men moving toward him, his arm outstretched. He tried not to think about what was coming. Then he realized that the Iroquois was snatching at the

Lamb of God medal he wore around his neck, though he didn't know why he had kept it. He had turned his back on his childhood religion a long time ago.

But suddenly he had an idea. "Don't touch that!" he shouted with whatever strength he possessed, momentarily startling the warrior into hesitating. The sky was growing dark, a storm was moving in quickly, but the Iroquois seemed too caught up in their rituals to have noticed.

His spirits rose. Perhaps he could count on divine intervention to save him after all.

Introduction

Étienne Brûlé is an enigma in the rollicking saga of Canada.

He had the most fantastic adventures and experiences, but we learn about them only second-hand, if we learn about them at all. He may have done amazing things we've never heard of. Then again, he may have been credited with exploits he had never heard of.

We don't know what he looked like. Sketches of him are merely artists' renderings, drawn from their own imaginations. We have no idea whether he suffered bouts of loneliness, grumbled about his boss, laughed uproariously or chuckled quietly. But we catch glimpses of him here and there. Like sunlight dancing through dense foliage, Brûlé the man flickers to life at unexpected moments and delights us.

His tale is as tantalizing for its gaps and contradictions as for its dramatic content. To unravel the mystery of Étienne Brûlé is to play detective, gathering eyewitness testimony, hearsay, and circumstantial evidence. We struggle to sort fact from fiction, weed out false witnesses, and consider the source and motive behind every assertion.

Étienne Brûlé

Brûlé himself seems to have left no written record of his experiences. Yet Samuel de Champlain expected him to make regular reports on the regions he was exploring, and there were long stretches of time when verbal accounts would have been impossible. It would appear that Champlain, like an author hiring a researcher, regarded Brûlé's reports as raw data that he incorporated into his own manuscripts, then discarded.

As a result, we see Étienne Brûlé filtered through the eyes of others, primarily Champlain and a few missionaries. We have to look for him in the background of their personal dramas, a minor bit player rarely noticed. When they got around to recording events, usually long after the fact, they were intent on making themselves look good, and couldn't help shading their accounts with their own prejudices, purposes, and vanities. They were capable of spreading gross misinformation, and in some instances Brûlé seems to have been the one who mischievously supplied it. The time came when no one, at least no Frenchman, wanted to praise him for anything, so whatever small credit he received was given grudgingly. And we never hear his side of the story.

Yet his name and stature as one of the players in the pageant of Canadian history survive to this day.

As a self-promoter, he was hopeless.

As an adventurer, he was unparalleled.

Chapter 1
A New Life Beckons

onfleur was a turmoil of activity in the spring of 1608. The frenetic comings and goings in the busy seaport on France's Normandy coast were typical of any harbour, but in April of this particular year a special excitement charged the atmosphere. Samuel de Champlain was about to lead a new expedition to the St. Lawrence River in Canada — his first to that region in five years — and establish a new colony there.

Étienne Brûlé was 16 that year, but somehow he had talked his way onto Champlain's team of carpenters and artisans, farmers and seamen, fur merchants and

A map of New France from 1597 showing the poor
knowledge of the area prior to 1600.

soldiers of fortune on their way to New France.

Brûlé had left his home village of Champigny-sur-
Marne, just south of Paris, in his early teens for reasons
no one knows, but it is easy to imagine the teenager
deciding there had to be a better life out there somewhere than the peasant-farming existence he had been
slated for.

Yet the stories he had heard about New France seemed too fantastic to be true. Native peoples travelling long distances in frail boats made of papery tree bark? Forests where a man could hunt without being arrested for poaching? Warriors who hacked off a vanquished enemy's scalp and displayed it like a trophy?

Étienne Brûlé wanted to see it all for himself, and his ticket to the spectacle would be Samuel de Champlain.

A Formidable Plan

Honfleur's expert carpenters had pre-built all the sections of the fortress and living quarters to be called "The Habitation," ready to be assembled at a settlement site Champlain had earmarked during a fact-finding mission back in 1603. That site would become Québec City. Extra lumber, window casings, and carpenters' tools were hauled aboard his ships, along with weapons, cannon, and box after box of everyday provisions for the settlers.

Two vessels were bound for the St. Lawrence River. Champlain, commander of the expedition, would take the helm of one ship during the voyage, then remain in New France through the winter to oversee the fledgling colony. He would be risking his life, and the lives of anyone who went with him. The survival rate for

Frenchmen who stayed in Canada after the last supply ship sailed away in early autumn had, so far, been pathetically low.

The captain of the other ship was François Gravé, Sieur du Pont, usually referred to as Pontgravé. An experienced fur merchant, he was charged with reviving the old trading post at Tadoussac and re-establishing the French presence on the St. Lawrence. Ideally, he would spend the summer bartering with the Native peoples, then return to France with both ships loaded with furs.

The two men were agents of a company that had negotiated with Henri IV, King of France, for a one-year monopoly in the fur trade, which meant that by royal decree no one else was allowed to traffic in pelts in New France during that period. In return for the privilege, the company had agreed to provide financing for exploration of the country and the establishment of settlements and missionary outposts to spread Christianity to the Native peoples.

The system made sense in theory, but in practice it created constant instability. Monopolies could be revoked as well as granted, and often were. Conversely, the companies who held them tended to be slow to honour all the conditions of their agreement, and with good reason.

In the first place, they had to deal with the Native

peoples, who were experts at getting what they wanted from the European newcomers before doling out information about their homelands or trading routes. What they usually wanted was military support for their intertribal wars.

As for the proposed colonies, the problem was that the settlers kept dying of things like scurvy, dysentery, and starvation, which made it difficult to attract new recruits. A person had to be desperate for a new life, addicted to danger or downright naïve to board a ship bound for the New World.

Étienne Brûlé might well have been all three.

The Adventure Begins

On April 5, Pontgravé's ship left Honfleur, sails billowing in the breeze as he set his course for the St. Lawrence River.

Eight days later Champlain followed in the second ship, with Étienne Brûlé aboard. As the younger man inhaled the sharp tang of the sea air, he must have had a huge grin on his face. He was only an indentured servant, an errand boy for Champlain, but he was on his way to the New World. Nothing else mattered.

The voyage might have given him second thoughts. Even on placid seas the endless expanse of water with no land in sight for days on end would be daunting to a former farm boy, and the North Atlantic in April has never been known for its tranquillity. Still, Brûlé would soon take to the thrill of shooting rapids in a birchbark canoe as if he had been born to it, so it is reasonable to assume he didn't spend much time with his head over the side of the ship.

During the crossing he would have been kept busy with chores, doing odd jobs for the commander, and getting to know his shipmates. One of them was an 18-year-old named Nicolas Marsolet.

Arriving at the Grand Banks on May 15, the ship acquired a playful escort when whales and dolphins swam alongside it, amusing the weary voyagers with their antics. The water was teeming with cod and the sky with screeching, diving seabirds. Whalers and cod-fishing boats were everywhere, manned by Basques from southwestern France and northern Spain, by Normans and Bretons, and by mariners from England and Ireland. The competition for the New World's marine resources was fierce. The competition for its other riches was just beginning.

Eleven days later, Champlain's crew sighted Newfoundland; three more days took them to Percé Rock and Gaspé.

The ship at last sailed into the St. Lawrence River, and as it advanced upstream, Brûlé caught sight of an enormous wilderness of forests, mountain ranges, and swamps. The river itself, little changed since its formation after the Ice Age, was 1300 kilometres of waterway known informally as the "River of Canada."

On June 3, the travellers reached the mouth of the Saguenay River and anchored outside the harbour at Tadoussac, unable to enter the port because of unfavourable winds and tides.

Squatters Cause Trouble
Champlain lowered a longboat from the ship so that he could head into the harbour and find out whether Pontgravé had arrived safely. He was only partway to shore when he spied a shallop approaching his longboat. As the small, sail-equipped rowing craft came closer, he saw two men manning it. One of them was Pontgravé's pilot.

They brought news, and it wasn't good. Pontgravé had arrived in New France safely enough, but the volatile fur trader had clashed almost immediately with Spanish Basques who had settled into the abandoned French trading post at Tadoussac. The Basques were trading furs in defiance of the monopoly held by Champlain's backers.

Pontgravé had ordered them to stop. According to the king's edict, he would have been within his legal rights to confiscate their ship, supplies, arms, and merchandise as punishment for disobeying the rules of the monopoly, but the Basques hadn't been overly impressed with the king's edict or the threat.

They had fired on Pontgravé's ship with their cannon and a shower of musket-shot, severely wounding the captain and three of his men, one of whom had since died. Then the Spaniards had boarded his vessel and had taken all the cannon and smaller arms, saying they would restore his property when they were ready to head back to Europe. Meanwhile they kept him, his ship, munitions, and men "in a state of security."

In other words, Pontgravé was a virtual prisoner.

Furthermore, they declared, they intended to keep right on trading for furs. What did a French king's command matter to them?

It was an ominous start to the summer's trading season, and Champlain knew he had to handle it with a judicious blend of firmness and diplomacy. After negotiating for access to his partner, he found Pontgravé badly hurt, but strong enough to discuss their options — their very limited options. A monopoly was only as effective as the power to back it up, and at the moment they didn't have a lot of power.

They decided on a compromise. They would agree not to take any action against the Basques for what they had done if, in turn, the Basques would honour the monopoly. In future, these disagreements would be referred to the French courts.

The captain of the Basque crew seems to have gone along with these terms, perhaps because he was a little intimidated by the fact that Champlain's ship was anchored just outside the harbour. He didn't know how many armed men might be on board, ready to launch an attack. And he was a whaler by profession, not a fur merchant. Trading for pelts was just a sideline. He wouldn't have wanted to end up losing his whaling rights because of one rash act.

With a crisis averted, Champlain made arrangements to have his partner cared for, then returned to his ship.

An Enthusiastic Reception
Champlain barely had a chance to catch his breath before the riverbank suddenly came to life with men, women, and children leaping into a fleet of canoes and pushing off from shore to race toward the French ship.

Brûlé must have been flabbergasted at the sight. He wouldn't have seen canoes before. They looked as if they would sink under the weight of a kitten, yet they supported anywhere from two full-grown adults to whole families, up to 30 people in the larger ones. They flew over the surface of the water with unparalleled speed and grace.

The canoes drew up to the ship and the Native peoples clambered aboard, eager to greet the French commander they still remembered from his visit five years earlier. These were the Montagnais, named mountaineers for the hilly lands they called home. The men, lean and muscular, were naked from the waist up, their bodies tattooed, their faces painted with bold slashes of colour. Some of the men wore their hair long and straight, some shaved half their head bald. Others had just a stiff, bristly ridge right down the centre of their crown, from forehead to nape.

The women were neither tattooed nor painted. Their skin was burnished to a golden brown, their dark hair oiled to a glossy sheen and worn straight and long. Their clothing was simple, made of animal skins, skimming over lithe bodies. Necklaces of shells and beads were their only decorations.

Undoubtedly the dark-eyed beauties caught and held Brûlé's gaze, making his heart beat just a little faster: he was 16 years old and he had been at sea for weeks.

Where The River Narrows
After the Montagnais left the ship, Champlain began

preparations for the final leg of the journey. Tadoussac was not the site he had chosen for his settlement. He had pinpointed a better spot, farther up the river.

He sent a crew of men ashore and set them to work building a 12-tonne craft called a pinnace, big enough to carry provisions, small enough to negotiate the upper reaches of the St. Lawrence.

Knowing it would take until the end of June to construct the boat, he decided to use the time to revisit the Saguenay, part of which he had explored briefly in 1603. While he was there, local Native peoples insisted that rapids and waterfalls turned the upper river into an obstacle course, and he wouldn't want to try to explore it on his own. But they casually mentioned an inland sea to the north, and he filed that bit of information in the back of his mind to look into when he had more time.

He returned to Tadoussac, found the pinnace ready to go, and set out up the St. Lawrence on the last day of June. The crew enjoyed some salmon fishing along the way, and Champlain dubbed the islands and capes they passed with names still in use 400 years later.

For Étienne Brûlé, this cruise was the beginning of a lifelong addiction to adventure travel that would take him to places even his illustrious commander would never see.

The day the expedition arrived at its destination

would be remembered for centuries to come, yet Champlain gives no indication in his journal that he thought July 3, 1608 was more significant than any other. He simply relates how he set the crew to work clearing the site for The Habitation.

Still, the moment when the fleur-de-lis was unfurled at Québec — a native word that means, "where the river narrows" — was the moment of the true birth of New France, with Samuel de Champlain as the proud father.

And Étienne Brûlé would experience his share of the labour pangs.

Chapter 2
The Habitation

Champlain worked his people hard. One crew was assigned to cutting down the butternut trees that covered the settlement site. Another group had to saw the trees into planks, while a third team dug a cellar and a moat, all in busy preparation for constructing lodgings, a storehouse, and even a pigeon-house.

As part of the work party, Étienne Brûlé would soon discover what it meant to be bone-weary.

When the building was completed, Champlain urged the men to plant crops so they could store up food for the winter, and he set an example by choosing a plot on the west side of the fort and starting his own garden.

The Habitation consisted of three main buildings, each two stories high. Galleries stretched around the upper floor living quarters, useful in the event of an attack. Space was set aside front and back for gardens, and a stockade and moat surrounded the whole complex. Access was by way of a drawbridge, and platforms were set up inside for cannon.

A small crew went back to Tadoussac with the pinnace for supplies, Brûlé and his friend Marsolet almost certainly among them. As the rookies on the team, they would be assigned to menial jobs such as carting boxes of provisions.

It was while they were gone that Champlain and his infant settlement faced their first lethal threat.

Mutiny Thwarted

One of the settlers, a man named Jean Duval, had started to hatch a plot when he saw the Spanish Basques at Tadoussac. Figuring they would pay good money to get rid of Champlain, he decided to assassinate his commander and hand over Québec to the Basques. He enlisted four others in his scheme by feeding them lies that discredited Champlain and by telling them they could make a fortune if they threw in their lot with the Spaniards.

These four, in turn, promised to win everyone else

over to their side so Champlain would be left isolated and vulnerable. After making a pact not to betray each other on pain of death, they launched a whispered campaign of innuendoes and threats that soon had the rest of the settlers in a state of terrified confusion.

The plotters planned to carry out their scheme before the supply vessel returned from Tadoussac, but one of the men had second thoughts. When a different pinnace of the trading company showed up first, the frightened conspirator quietly told its captain what was going on. The captain took the story to Champlain, making sure the informant would be pardoned.

With his usual no-nonsense efficiency, Champlain had the ringleaders seized and put in chains, then faced the rest of the settlers with the facts, offering a pardon to those who would agree to tell him everything they knew about the conspiracy. He took their depositions in writing in front of witnesses, ordered handcuffs made for the authors of the plot, and had the men transported to Tadoussac to be held there until a trial could be arranged.

Étienne Brûlé must have been disappointed if indeed he was part of the crew that had gone to Tadoussac for provisions. He had missed all the excitement.

However, he would have been in Québec in time

for the event that became North America's first recorded trial.

And he definitely witnessed the ghoulish outcome.

A Traitor's Punishment

When Pontgravé returned the prisoners to Québec, Champlain's witnesses were afraid the plotters would wangle a pardon somehow and then be free to take their revenge. They needn't have worried. Duval's co-conspirators were found guilty and sent off to France to be dealt with. Duval was convicted and condemned to death, and the sentence was carried out in the new little colony of Québec, dramatically and without delay. He was hanged and beheaded, and his severed head was impaled on the end of a pike, which was set up in the highest part of the fort as a warning to anybody else who might entertain treasonous thoughts.

Pontgravé returned to France as planned, and Champlain remained at The Habitation to nurture his settlement through the winter. It wasn't long before everything was back to normal and he was able to report, "All who remained conducted themselves correctly in the discharge of their duty."

With Duval's macabre head presiding over the chastened community, it is difficult to imagine them doing otherwise.

The Habitation

A Grim Winter

As work on The Habitation continued, Brûlé and Marsolet did their share of the hard labour, but they found time to visit with the Montagnais and learn a bit of their language.

Like the neighbouring Algonquin of the area around the Ottawa River, the Montagnais were hunter-gatherers. Travelling in small bands, they fished for eels and hunted porcupine, beaver, moose, caribou, and bear. If the summer's hunt and eel catches were good, they could trade their extras for corn and other sustenance to help them through the winter. If not, they had to hope the winter hunt would be better.

The summer of 1608 hadn't been a good one for the Montagnais. Game had been scarce, and so had eels. Mohawk warriors had harassed the Montagnais and raided their villages, making off with their food stores and whatever pelts they had managed to gather. The Montagnais were now too frightened to venture out along the trade routes.

Several Montagnais bands gathered at the Québec settlement in mid-September and asked Champlain to take care of their provisions in The Habitation's storehouse. They wanted to stay inside the fortress, at least at night, but Champlain opened the gates only for the women and children. The men had to stay outside the walls and be satisfied with the comfort of having armed Frenchmen nearby if they were attacked.

Frost arrived early in October, and the trees lost most of their leaves within a couple of weeks. Brutal winds hit hard in November, and around the middle of the month a heavy snowfall brought the lakes and rivers to flood levels. The last beaver hunt of the season was a failure.

Several Montagnais and two of Champlain's men died of dysentery from eating badly cooked eels. By Christmas Champlain had to release the Native peoples' provisions, but there was enough food for only three or four weeks more.

The Montagnais left to try again to hunt beaver and elk, but returned in February, exhausted, defeated, and emaciated. They appeared on the south shore of the iced-up river, and when they tried to cross an opening to get to the settlement, the ice closed in, trapping and smashing their canoes to smithereens. The refugees managed to jump to a large block of ice, some of the women carrying children on their backs. They drifted toward the north shore where, by an incredible stroke of luck, they were hit by another ice floe with such force the people were thrown onto the land.

At the fort they were given bread and beans, but there simply wasn't enough food for everyone. Ready to try anything, the settlers took the body of a dog that had died and hung it in a tree, hoping to lure some wild game, but the starving people were so desperate, they chopped down the tree and devoured the carcass raw.

By late February the settlement had also endured a two-day blizzard and everyone, French and Native peoples alike, was on the brink of starvation. Somehow they managed to keep going, scrimping by on tiny rations of gruel, but scurvy hit and lasted until mid-April, afflicting 18 men and killing 10. Champlain sent out men to find a certain fir tree used by native women decades earlier for a potion that had saved some of Jacques Cartier's men. But no one knew which tree it was or how the mixture had been made, and the searchers didn't come up with anything that worked.

The term of the company's monopoly had expired in January, and the future of the colony looked bleak. By the time spring made its appearance, only 7 of the 28 men Champlain had brought with him from France were still alive. There was little they could do but wait for relief ships to arrive.

Somehow Étienne Brûlé and Nicolas Marsolet lived through that terrible winter, perhaps because they were young and strong, or perhaps because they were lucky.

Whether their luck would hold through the hairraising adventures ahead remained to be seen.

Chapter 3
Tribal Wars

tienne Brûlé was only one year older than he had been when he boarded the ship that took him to the New World, but the events of that year had toughened and matured him. He had been tested to the limit of his endurance and had triumphed simply by surviving.

He and Marsolet had picked up enough of the Montagnais language to know they had a talent that could be useful. And they weren't raw recruits any more. They were seasoned veterans.

But they had yet to experience the thrill and terror of facing a painted Mohawk on the warpath.

Shortly after the break-up of the ice on the St.

Lawrence, a party of Algonquin from the regions of the St. Maurice and Ottawa Rivers arrived at Québec with their furs. While they were pleased to see the new trading post, they warned Champlain that the Mohawk or one of the other Iroquois nations would try to destroy it.

Champlain and others had promised military support to fight the five nations of the Iroquois League for years, but had yet to engage in a single battle. Now there was an intriguing new wrinkle. The Huron Confederacy had joined the Algonquin–Montagnais alliance. This presented an opportunity for Champlain to develop more contacts.

He was beginning to hear the beat of war drums, but with his decimated ranks and depleted supplies, he didn't have many resources to contribute to a military offensive.

The Politics of War

On June 5, 1609, a ship finally arrived from France with supplies and personnel. Its captain was Pontgravé's nephew, who said his uncle was on the way to the settlement and would arrive any day. The young captain also brought news that Champlain was expected to head back to France in the very near future to report to the company directors on his progress.

With all the trouble the colony had faced over the

past year, Champlain didn't have much progress to report. He hadn't explored new territory, hadn't penetrated into the interior to find new trading partners, and as yet couldn't boast that his settlement at Québec would last through a second winter. It had barely scraped through the first.

He headed for Tadoussac to confer with Pontgravé. They decided that Champlain should make an excursion up the St. Lawrence to meet with the leaders of their native allies, taking with him a force made up of whatever men they could spare from Québec and Tadoussac.

Was Brûlé part of Champlain's force? It seems likely. Champlain had only a small pool of men to draw from in Québec. It is hard to believe he would have left behind the young, strong, fighting-trim Brûlé, who had acquired the rudiments of a native language.

Pontgravé stayed in Tadoussac while Champlain and his crew sailed up the St. Lawrence in mid-June. Close to the River of the Iroquois, later to be known as the Richelieu, they came upon a large encampment of Algonquin and Huron.

This encounter was a first for both the Huron and the French, and they undoubtedly checked each other out very thoroughly. Each wanted something from the other, and each was prepared to offer something in return.

The Huron lived around Georgian Bay on Lake Huron, one of the great western "seas" Champlain had heard about from time to time, and were successful farmers who bartered agricultural products for pelts and other goods. They had developed a network of trade routes that extended their reach deep into the continent in all directions and made them brokers for the merchandise of many tribes. As far back as 1603, Champlain had learned that the Huron were trading with the Algonquin for French wares. A connection with them would be a major breakthrough he could report to his directors.

An important Algonquin chief named Iroquet and some of his people had spent the winter with the Huron and had invited one of its headmen, Ochasteguin, to take part in a raid against the Mohawk, along with their promised ally, Champlain.

Ochasteguin had accepted, eager to meet the French and trade with them directly. And fighting side by side with them to drive the Mohawk out of the St. Lawrence Valley would enhance his own prestige.

Champlain, in turn, was delighted to meet Ochasteguin, welcoming his participation in the war plans. There was no better way to solidify relationships with native trading partners than to show goodwill by helping them with their battles.

As was their custom, the leaders of the native alliance welcomed Champlain into their wigwams and presented him with their best pelts. The exchange of gifts was an integral part of their trading ritual.

The next day Champlain returned their hospitality, inviting them onto his shallop. While the Huron and Algonquin warriors waited on shore in full battle array, their headmen sat quietly smoking their pipes. After a long, meditative silence, one of the chiefs stood and addressed the whole assembly in a booming voice, giving a stirring rally-the-troops oration and recalling Champlain's long-standing promise to help them fight their enemies.

Champlain responded with a demonstration of the French weaponry he would use against the Mohawk. He raised his *arquebus*, a heavy musket, and fired it. Then several of his men fired theirs in a booming explosion that echoed over the water.

The audience was thoroughly impressed and all agreed that they were looking forward to seeing these marvellous thunder-sticks used against the Mohawk.

It would have seemed natural to head straight up the Richelieu into Iroquois territory right from there, but the Native people first wanted to go back to Québec to trade for goods, see the buildings the French had constructed, and prepare for war with their traditional ceremonies and feasts. To them, the lead-up to a battle was as important as the battle itself.

Eager to maintain the friendly mood, Champlain said he was happy to oblige, and promised to put on an even better demonstration of firepower when they reached The Habitation.

The feasting was supposed to last for three days, but three days stretched into six.

A Clash of Cultures

Two shallops were provisioned for the foray into Mohawk territory, Champlain's and the one that had come up from Tadoussac as reinforcement, commanded by Pontgravé. The war party finally set out early in July, but along the way, Pontgravé apparently traded all his goods, decided his work was finished, and went back to Tadoussac. By the time the remaining shallop reached the Richelieu, Champlain's contingent consisted of only nine Frenchmen — not exactly the strong force their native allies had been led to expect.

Champlain was surprised when most of the Algonquin kept on going past the Richelieu, heading home with their European goods. It seemed they had never planned to be part of the war party. There were now 60 warriors, not quite the 300-strong war party the French had hoped for.

The heady euphoria of the expedition's beginnings gradually dissipated and the action slowed to a crawl. Shortly after the reduced force started up the Richelieu they paused for two days to take advantage of the excellent hunting and fishing of the area. Champlain, a scientific observer at heart, was content to take soundings of the river and make notes about the flora and fauna of the countryside.

Eventually, the group set out again, but when they reached the Chambly Rapids, Champlain's shallop could go no farther. He was thoroughly annoyed at his travelling companions for not warning him about this obstacle, but they couldn't see the problem. The rapids were perfectly navigable for them. Of course, they were travelling in canoes.

Champlain barked out an order for his people to take the shallop and go back to the mouth of the river. He would carry on with the Native people by himself in one of their canoes, unless any of the other Frenchmen wanted to volunteer to go with him.

Only two stepped forward.

The Montagnais insisted that because they were the oldest and closest allies of the French, Champlain should travel in their canoes, not with the Huron or Algonquin. He went along with their protocol while the other two Frenchmen portaged around the rough

waters with the 60 warriors, carrying 24 canoes.
They continued southward for 17 days.

Battle Preparations

Each evening the war party set up an encampment.
Some of the men erected bark-covered wigwams, others
took the brand new axes they had obtained at the Québec
trading session and chopped down trees for a barricade.
They placed it around the whole perimeter of the
encampment except the shoreline, where they left their
canoes ready in case they needed to make a quick exit.

Another group went off in three canoes to recon-
noitre, and if they saw no sign of the Mohawk in a radius
of several kilometres, they reported back that it was safe
to go to sleep for the night.

Champlain urged the native leaders to post sen-
tries, but they said they had worked hard enough and
needed their rest.

First, though, they had some rituals to attend to.
They set up a shaman's shaking tent ceremony to pre-
dict the movements of their enemy. Champlain's journal
described what followed. The naked shaman inside the
tent shook one of the poles and muttered incanta-
tions to invoke the devil and find out how the battle
would end. After a while, wrote Champlain, the shaman
leapt to his feet, shouting and writhing until he had

worked himself into a sweat while the tribe sat around the tent watching, enraptured. He used a loud, eerie voice and an unfamiliar language and said it was the devil talking.

Regarding the entire ritual as base trickery, Champlain recorded that he did his best to put a stop to it. "These scoundrels go on deceiving these poor people just to get things from them," he railed.

It was probably a good thing he was delivering his harangue in French, so the Huron either didn't understand him at all or his Montagnais interpreter softened his words. Otherwise, the budding friendship might have fallen apart right then and there. Fortunately, a young man was waiting in the wings to take over as a more culturally sensitive diplomat, but his appearance on the stage of Franco-Huron relations was a year away. Even if Étienne Brûlé was on the scene for the shaman's ceremony, he was in no position to tell his commander to mind his manners.

Champlain was on more familiar ground when the chiefs took sticks, one for each warrior, and used them to arrange the order of battle formation. Then they called their warriors together and drilled them according to the plan.

Finally, everyone settled in for the night.

The war party set off again in the morning and

eventually entered the Grande Isle Channel. Suddenly, the Frenchmen's eyes widened as they stared at the largest inland lake they had ever seen.

The Huron weren't impressed. They said the lakes where they came from were much, much bigger.

Champlain shrugged off their boasts and bestowed his own name on the body of water.

The party proceeded with great caution, still moving south, now travelling only by night and staying hidden in the forest in the daytime. They didn't light fires, so their meals consisted of corn meal soaked in cold water. They began to pay attention to dreams and their possible import. Champlain, trying a new tack, began reporting dreams that could be interpreted only as imminent victory.

They were near present-day Point Ticonderoga late in the evening on July 29 when they sighted a cluster of canoes made of elm bark. The native scouts told Champlain that only the Iroquois used clumsy elm bark canoes.

The enemies had found each other.

Rules of Engagement

Champlain had taken part in many battles in his life, but none like this one. He was accustomed to a certain dignity and seriousness in warfare, with tidy lines of men marching toward their foes, or alternatively, using the element of surprise to catch the enemy off guard.

The native adversaries ran at each other, issuing challenges accompanied by jeers and war songs. Then both sides abruptly backed off. The Mohawk headed for shore and started building a rough barricade while their enemies clustered their canoes in deep water offshore, held them together with long poles, and hunkered down to wait until it was time for the skirmish to begin.

When all these preparations had been completed, the two sides sent out envoys to make sure they both still wanted to fight.

Champlain couldn't believe it. He had considered the battle a foregone conclusion. Once war was declared, a French army didn't change its mind at the last minute and go home.

He must have been relieved when word came back that combat would begin at daybreak, when the sun could witness the warriors' valour.

Throughout the night, both groups continued trading insults and singing at the tops of their voices, each shouting to the other how humiliated they were going to be the next morning, and exchanging mutual accusations that suggested they actually knew each other on a personal basis. Obviously, they had been up against these opponents before.

A depiction of Champlain's first encounter with the Iroquois
in 1609 on the shores of the future Lake Champlain

It was a raucous few hours, and in Champlain's opinion it was no way to wage a proper campaign.

Even so, he did have one surprise in store for the Mohawk. After explaining his strategy to the allied chiefs, he and the other two Frenchman used the cover of darkness to steal ashore and hide in the woods.

The Skirmish Begins
As soon as the first glimmers of dawn began to streak across the sky, Champlain and his two stalwarts put on

their armour and plumed helmets, then poured powder and ball into their weapons. Champlain stuffed four bullets into his *arquebus.*

The attackers moved in on the shore and 200 Mohawk emerged from behind their barricade. Champlain described them later as strong and robust, led by three chiefs, and he couldn't help admiring how slowly and calmly they advanced to meet their fate.

They had reason to be calm. They were used to winning.

The Huron, Algonquin, and Montagnais landed, leapt out of their canoes, and started racing toward the Mohawk, who stayed close to their fort.

When the attackers were within striking distance, they parted ranks and Champlain strode into the gap, sun glinting off his armour, *arquebus* at his side. Clearly he had planned his entrance for maximum dramatic impact, and it had the desired effect.

The Mohawk froze, staring in blank amazement at the sight of a Frenchman in full battle gear. But after only a few seconds, they recovered their wits and drew their bows.

Champlain raised his *arquebus* and took aim at the three chiefs, who had been pointed out to him by the Montagnais. The chiefs were wearing wooden body armour, but the four bullets of Champlain's first shot killed two of them instantly and mortally wounded the third.

Wild shouting filled the air as thick volleys of arrows began flying on both sides. While Champlain was reloading his weapon, the other two Frenchmen in the woods fired their muskets. The Mohawk shields of hemp and wood were no defence against this kind of assault, and those who hadn't fallen stampeded away, their attackers in close pursuit.

Champlain fired again, taking down still more men. The skirmish was over within moments, leaving some 50 Mohawk dead, including 2 chiefs, and 10 or 12 taken prisoner. Champlain's men and their allies, having suffered only a few minor casualties, looted the camp, taking large amounts of corn along with the Mohawks' discarded suits of armour.

Those Mohawks who had managed to get away would spread the word to the rest of the Iroquois Nation that a new kind of warfare had come to their country.

And they would adapt to it all too quickly.

The Victorious Aftermath
At their encampment that night the victors tortured their prisoners with a terrible cruelty that left the Frenchmen shaken, even though they must have seen atrocities of equal brutality in Europe. The French

would nod approvingly over the torture of a traitor or heretic, but they had rules about the treatment of prisoners of war.

The Native peoples had rules, too. They were just vastly different.

At one point, Champlain offered to shoot one half-dead victim, but the native guards refused to allow it. He turned on his heel and started to stalk away. Realizing he was angry, they decided to mollify him. He was allowed to put the prisoner out of his misery.

In his journal, Champlain meticulously recorded every gruesome detail, but paid homage to the vanquished warriors, whose stoicism was such that even under the most unspeakable torments they "appeared to have felt nothing at all."

A few hours after the celebrations, the victors were on their way home with their surviving prisoners, who sang their warrior chants the whole distance to keep up their spirits, under no illusions about what they were facing.

Was Étienne Brûlé a witness to all these dramas? It seems likely, but even if not, his chance would come soon enough.

Homeward Bound
The war party broke up at the Chambly Rapids on the

Richelieu. Ochasteguin and Iroquet vowed to return the following year with 400 warriors for another raid on the Mohawk and promised that afterwards they would take Champlain to their own country and farther north, where there were copper mines.

Champlain readily agreed to rendezvous with them in a year at the mouth of the Richelieu. He then headed for Tadoussac with the Montagnais.

As the returning warriors entered the port, they sang a triumphal song and waved sticks on which they had hung the scalps and beads taken from the warriors they had killed.

The Montagnais women stripped off their clothes and swam naked to the canoes to receive the trophies, which they draped around their necks like ornaments. Then they went back to shore and danced until they exhausted themselves. More feasting and celebrating followed, with gifts brought to Champlain and apologies offered by those who hadn't taken part in the battle.

Champlain returned to Québec and carried on with improvements to The Habitation, while the settlers began making preparations for their second winter in New France. When it was time for him to sail for France, he felt he had some solid accomplishments to report.

He appointed an overseer for the Québec settlement and left him with detailed instructions for avoiding the problems of the previous winter. Then on September 5, Champlain and Pontgravé sailed for France, satisfied that they had done all they could to ensure the survival of the colony.

As Étienne Brûlé and his companions watched the ships disappear over the horizon, they must have wondered if they would be alive to see them return in the spring.

Chapter 4
The Turning Point

he second winter in Québec was easier than the first, and Étienne Brûlé spent much of it with the Montagnais, ranging through their mountainous terrain and living at least part of the time as they lived.

With Champlain in France and no one else reporting events in the settlement, the clues to Étienne Brûlé's life become more difficult to find. However, some conclusions about how he spent those months are self-evident, and when the official accounts pick up again we see him with a whole new set of skills.

It is certain he would have basked in the sensual delights of an autumn in the St. Lawrence Valley, when the sun was warm on the skin and the oppressive humidity of summer had lifted, leaving the air crisp and sweet-smelling. The leaves changed from cool shades of green to a blaze of reds and yellows and russets, lending an almost ethereal sense of lightness to the dense forests. The woods abounded in wild game, the streams and lakes with fish. The crops and gardens that had been planted in the settlement were ripe for harvesting. The thick swarms of mosquitoes were gone, so a day in the woods or on the water was pure pleasure.

Brûlé learned to use a bow and arrow for hunting, and was expected to skin and dress whatever quarry he brought down. Because the Montagnais were nomads, their ability to find their way through large tracts of rugged country was honed to a fine art, and their knowledge rubbed off on their visitor.

He acquired the rudiments of navigating a canoe, catching the rhythm that would let him paddle for hours without stopping. He learned to endure long sessions of kneeling in the flimsy confines of the craft, back ramrod straight, just like his native mentors. The birchbark canoe was light and responsive, but fragile, and accidents were an ever-present possibility. In later years, a missionary would write: "In this craft, one is always within an inch of death but for the thickness of five or six layers of paper."

The Turning Point

Over the winter, Brûlé discovered that the season most dreaded by settlers could be the best time to hunt, with animals weakened from hunger leaving their tracks in the deep snow. He learned to travel on snowshoes, an ingenious native innovation made by bending hickory to form a racquet-shaped frame and weaving it with a netting made of sinew, hide, or twine.

By spring, he had re-invented himself. He had prepared himself for something.

He just wasn't sure yet what that something was.

A Hero's Welcome
Spring arrived early in the St. Lawrence Valley in 1610, and the Québec colony was thriving — good news for Champlain when he arrived after a discouraging winter in France. He had tried his best to get the monopoly license renewed, but without luck.

He and Pontgravé had left Honfleur early in March. Bad weather drove Champlain's ship to England before it was out of the Channel. When he started out again after several days, the vessel was blown back to France. The voyage had to be aborted when the usually healthy Champlain took sick, delaying the trip for more than a month. When he set sail for the third time, he still felt weak, but flatly refused to wait any longer.

Joining Pontgravé in Tadoussac, Champlain was

greeted by a crowd of waiting Montagnais warriors who sent up a shout of welcome for the man who had led them to such a resounding victory over the Mohawk. Even before he went ashore they were thumping for an encore.

He met with the Montagnais leaders, assuring them that he was ready and willing to go on the warpath with them again, but only on condition that they would make good on past promises to guide him to the "great inland salt sea" to the north. They agreed to do so, but not until the following year. He didn't argue. He had an alternative plan.

He had told the Huron and Algonquin the year before that he would help them in their wars if they would show him their country and the copper mines they had talked about.

Étienne Brûlé's chance to shine was coming closer.

On The Warpath Again

Sixty Montagnais warriors went ahead to Three Rivers, at the mouth of the St. Maurice River, and in mid-June Champlain and his men, including Étienne Brûlé, followed in four pinnaces loaded with merchandise for trading with the Algonquin and Huron.

Four hundred warriors were supposed to meet Champlain at St. Ignace Island, near the mouth of the

Richelieu River. He had chosen the location purposefully. He hoped that the region would become part of a new monopoly zone, or at the very least, that the free-lance traders who followed Champlain on his travels would not persist that far up the St. Lawrence.

The first hope was dashed by royal indifference before the expedition even started, and Champlain had underestimated the free-lancers. They trailed right behind his vessels, determined to grab their share of the business, and without a monopoly license, he had no right to stop them.

A few kilometres past Québec, a canoe carrying an Algonquin and a Montagnais intercepted Champlain's party and urged him to pick up speed and hurry on to Three Rivers to join up with their Montagnais relatives already there. They said that 200 Huron and Algonquin were at the rendezvous at St. Ignace Island, and 200 more were on their way.

The Algonquin messenger dangled a carrot in the form of a 30-centimetre strip of copper, which he presented to Champlain, saying there were large quantities of the metal to be found near the great inland lake to the west.

At Three Rivers, Champlain's group joined with the Montagnais, and they all headed on to the Richelieu together, though Champlain took only one of the pinnaces and left the others moored there.

The advance party reached St. Ignace Island and found it deserted. They learned from a scout that the Algonquin and Huron had already arrived, met up with 100 Mohawk, and summarily attacked them. The Mohawk had fought them off and were now barricaded in a hastily erected fortress a short distance up the Richelieu.

Champlain asked for volunteers to go ashore with him, but only four stepped forward, one of them undoubtedly Étienne Brûlé. Champlain doesn't mention Brûlé in his account of this expedition, but there is no reason why he should, any more than modern commanders name individual soldiers in their memoirs. And plunging headlong into danger was Brûlé's style. He wouldn't hang back in safety and endure the jeers of the Montagnais warriors.

Once ashore, Champlain's problem was that he had no idea where the Algonquin and Huron were. After their headlong rush into battle, they had disappeared. The exasperated commander and his intrepid followers started out through the forest to find their allies, slogging through swampy terrain with water up to their knees, mosquitoes buzzing around them in swarms so thick the men could barely see or breathe. For Champlain, the whole mission had degenerated into a comedy of errors.

Eventually their allies found them and guided Champlain and his men toward the enemy position. All at once they heard a shouted exchange of threats and insults, coming from just ahead.

A Terrible Victory

The Algonquin and Montagnais were fast runners. The French, burdened down with armour, tried to keep up with the race through the woods, but fell behind and got lost again. One of the warriors doubled back to find them and steered them in the right direction, but the men who had reached the fortress ahead of them had already launched another assault. They had lost some of their best men, and the Mohawk were still protected behind their thick wooden palisade.

When Champlain and his men finally caught up to the others at the battle site the commander directed the gunfire from behind the cover of the forest, but came within a hair's breadth of being killed when a Mohawk arrow split the tip of his ear and pierced his neck. He pulled out the arrow and continued firing. Another arrow found its mark in one of his men. Champlain pulled it out as well and resumed the battle.

It was clear that the Mohawk had learned a great deal from their single encounter with French weaponry the previous year. Victory was by no means assured.

Champlain directed the attackers to chop down a tree so it would fall on the fortress. He and his men advanced, firing their muskets at closer and closer range. When the tree crashed down and opened up a breech in the barricade, he shouted at the warriors to storm through it, then drew his sword and led the charge. The French were running out of ammunition, but at the crucial moment, reinforcements arrived from the pinnace.

Overwhelmed, the Mohawk tried to run, but of the 100 warriors, 15 were captured and the rest were killed.

The war party returned to St. Ignace Island and spent the rest of the day celebrating with singing and dancing.

Torture ceremonies began and went on for several days. When the grisly rituals finally ended, most prisoners were dead. Champlain stepped in at one point and bargained for the life of a Mohawk, taking him into French custody, an act of mercy he would come to regret.

Algonquin Chief Iroquet and his Huron friend Ochasteguin finally showed up with 80 men in fur-laden canoes, far short of the 200 warriors they had pledged. Then Champlain's traders arrived, their pinnaces loaded down with merchandise for barter. The free-lancers, like seagulls in the wake of a fishing trawler, were right behind them, eager to profit from a gathering of so many Native peoples.

Champlain remarked sourly that while he and his people had searched out new trading partners and had taken all the risks, these opportunists hadn't done anything but sit back and wait for their chance to reap the benefits.

The French spread out their wares and started trading, but the fierce competition gave the Algonquin and Huron the edge and they were quick to take advantage. They held back pelts, driving prices up to levels 16 to 18 times higher than they had been just two years earlier.

During the powwow held on St. Ignace Island, Champlain moved quietly among the Huron, suggesting that they rendezvous secretly with him the following year at the Lachine Rapids near Montréal Island, which would shorten their journey from the interior.

He then set in motion the plan that would alter the course of Étienne Brûlé's life forever.

Brûlé's Mission

Brûlé had been intrigued by the Algonquin and Huron and had told Champlain at some point that he would like to go with some of them to their homelands to learn more of their language and customs.

Champlain decided that the time had come to pursue the idea. During the gathering at St. Ignace Island, he and Pontgravé took Brûlé aside and asked him if he still was interested in heading off with the Native people. If so, they said, they would try to arrange it. He could observe the country and its rivers, find out about minerals and other resources, and perhaps travel to the fabled massive lake. It would be an important mission and they were careful to warn Brûlé that it wouldn't be easy. In case he didn't get the message, Champlain and Pontgravé graphically described all the things that could go wrong.

When Brûlé eagerly accepted in spite of this litany of potential doom, Champlain took the proposal to Iroquet, the Algonquin chief whose tribal lands bordered Huron territory.

Iroquet, eager to cement his relationship with the French, greeted Champlain's proposal with enthusiasm and promised to treat Brûlé as his own son. Champlain, believing they had made a firm deal, was pleased. "Keep your eyes open," he told Brûlé when giving him the news. "And on your return, make a good report of everything we could use."

But when the chief told the other leaders about the agreement, they weren't sure they liked the idea. They pointed out that if anything untoward happened to the youth, even by accident, the French might blame them and decide to avenge him.

Iroquet relayed the objections to Champlain, who demanded a meeting with all the chiefs and leaders. Angrily, he told them that if they went back on this agreement they could consider their friendship with him to be at an end. The chiefs were alarmed and insisted they were merely concerned about Brûlé's welfare. The dramatic change in his way of life and an unfamiliar diet might make him ill, they suggested. They didn't want problems with the lad to make Champlain turn against them.

Champlain assured them that Brûlé would adapt easily to his new life and was unlikely to become ill, and they wouldn't be held responsible for anything that went wrong unless they mistreated him.

Finally the two sides came up with a compromise. If Champlain would allow a young native man to accompany him to France, the Algonquin would take Brûlé home with them, probably to winter in Huronia, as they so often did. Everyone would reunite in the spring, when each youth would give an account of his experiences.

Champlain agreed to take Savignon, the younger brother of a Huron chief. He had wanted to get closer to the Huron people, and there could be no better way than to assume guardianship of one of their young men. And if Iroquet did winter with his friends, Brûlé would be regarded as the Hurons' guest of honour. It was a perfect arrangement.

Champlain had reason to be proud of his coup. He had put in place another building block in his plan for westward exploration and an expanded fur trade.

The Algonquin and Huron were just as pleased with themselves. The exchange of the two youths could lead to a truly personal link to the French, whose weapons made them powerful allies.

Étienne Brûlé must have been thrilled that his commander would put so much faith in him. He was just 18, and smart enough to know how untutored he was in the tricky art of diplomacy. But he also knew how important it could be for Champlain to be able to pull an interpreter from his own ranks instead of depending on native translators. If he played his cards right, he just might become indispensable to the commander.

Yet for all his pride and excitement, he must have had a twinge of doubt at the last minute. Étienne Brûlé watched everyone he had come to know over the past two years sail away, leaving him to fend for himself among strangers. He hadn't even begun to learn the Huron language, so different from the Montagnais. Even the Algonquin tongue was a dialect he was just beginning to learn. He was unfamiliar with the customs of these tribes and wasn't sure what they might expect of him. He had no idea where they lived, except that it was somewhere in the vast darkness beyond the known world. He would have no one to go to for help if these warriors turned against him, no mentor to guide him through a whole new way of life, no friend for comfort and companionship.

He had one chance, and one chance only, to change his mind. Once the French boats disappeared down the river, it would be too late for regrets.

He watched them go, then squared his shoulders and stepped into a birchbark canoe.

Chapter 5
Rising to
the Challenge

Brûlé didn't have much time for second-guessing. The journey ahead would be long and arduous, covering territory never before seen by any European, though for 6000 years various native groups had travelled the route he was about to "discover."

He must have been grateful for the opportunity over the past year at Québec to practise his canoeing and portaging skills and strengthen his body for the sheer physical effort that would be required of him. Simply keeping up with his experience-hardened companions would have been a daunting challenge, and undoubtedly he bedded down every night with excruciating stiffness in muscles he didn't know he had, only to wake up to a whole new set of aches and pains from sleeping on the damp ground.

His first test was to get past the obstacle that had stopped Jacques Cartier in his tracks and every French explorer since: the Rapids of Lachine.

We can't know beyond any doubt that Brûlé and the Huron shot those formidable rapids, but it is almost certain. The Native peoples routinely did it, and the temptation to test Brûlé's mettle would have been hard to resist. Besides, he was too eager for adventure to want to take the safer option and portage around the area.

The voyagers paddled up the Ottawa River, penetrating into the heart of the Canadian Shield, where immense mountains had been worn down over the ages to a vast, forbidding tableland, a crust of rock polished by ancient glaciers and carpeted by dense stands of conifers.

Brûlé took part in a ceremony at the Chaudière Falls, an offering of tobacco to the spirit of the turbulent waters to ensure their safe passage. He shared in the singing and dancing and heard the legends that had been passed down by the tribal elders.

Farther up the Ottawa River, the travellers turned up the Mattawa, the link to the western waterways. It led them to Lake Nipissing and, in turn, to the French River, sometimes a gently flowing river in a broad, tree-lined valley, sometimes a powerful torrent in a narrow, rocky gorge.

Hour after hour the quiet was broken only by the soft, sluicing sound of dipping paddles and the mocking laughter of loons. Occasionally Brûlé could look up and spy a black bear or a timber wolf watching the passing parade, or catch a glimpse of a startled white-tailed deer bounding away to take cover in the forest.

Rapids and waterfalls, mid-river shoals and islands, rocky outcroppings and weed-tangled bays — Brûlé learned to negotiate them all.

Then, at last, the voyagers emerged from their long, narrow passage into a broad expanse of sun-dappled water. They had reached what would one day be called Lake Huron.

For Étienne Brûlé, scruffy peasant from Île-de-France, errand boy for the Sieur de Champlain, this was a rebirth.

He had found his home.

A Devastating Setback

Just after reaching the settlement at Québec, Champlain received shocking news. His king was dead. Henri IV had been assassinated, stabbed to death by a religious extremist. In spite of his reluctance to grant a monopoly to the company Champlain worked for, he at least had shown sincere interest in the New France ventures. The new king was nine years old, and his mother, Marie de Medici, was acting as Regent. In terms of support for the colony, she was an unknown quantity.

Exhausted and still recovering from his wounds, Champlain was unsure of what he might be walking into when he faced the company directors in France in early August.

When he arrived, he found that his fears had been justified. His main ally in the consortium no longer enjoyed a special place in the inner circle of the court, and investors were backing off. Nevertheless, he managed to keep a few diehards on side and started preparing for his return to Québec.

He got married just after Christmas, seemingly for the dowry and the connections his new wife's family brought him. A hearts-and-flowers romance was unlikely. His new wife, Hélène Boullé, was only 12 years old, and Champlain was 43. The marriage was to be in name only for at least two years.

In March, he and Pontgravé headed back to New France, more determined than ever to prove their detractors wrong. The child bride wasn't along, but the Huron guest, Savignon, was aboard. The meeting to exchange the two young men, who in effect had acted as hostage for one another, would be one of the first priorities for Champlain.

The voyage was gruelling. Storms were frequent and so ferocious the voyagers seriously doubted they would survive. When they approached the Grand Banks they had to manoeuvre their way through giant icebergs and ice floes in fog and darkness before they reached safety. Even in less treacherous waters they faced hard going. The temperatures were so low the ship's rigging was frozen and covered with icicles, and the deck was a hazardous sheet of ice. It took them until May 13 to reach Tadoussac, which was still under a blanket of snow. It had been another harsh winter, and the Montagnais at Tadoussac were starving.

Dread Turns To Relief

Worried about the colony at Québec, Champlain headed there just a few days later, dreading what he might find. To his relief, the settlers had wintered comfortably. The stores they had set aside from the fall harvest, along with a good hunting season, had seen them through, and they were all set for the new season's trading and explorations.

Almost immediately, Champlain started up the St. Lawrence at the head of a flotilla, which included 13 pinnaces, to keep his appointment with the Huron at the Lachine Rapids.

When he reached Three Rivers, Champlain found his gaze drawn to the St. Maurice River and his thoughts drifted to the mysterious northern sea he had been told about.

He spoke to the local Algonquin chief and suggested that perhaps a native guide could lead a French crew up the river, but the chief flatly refused, citing the same excuses Champlain had heard from the Algonquin on the Saguenay.

What neither chief told Champlain was that their people had learned to use their strategic knowledge of their homelands to barter passage for goods, and they were not prepared to lose their economic advantages by opening up the territory to anyone else.

Champlain carried on to Lachine. Arriving eight days late for the rendezvous, he found no native encampment at the landing site on Montréal Island. Not sure whether he had missed his allies or they hadn't arrived yet, he decided to wait a while and use the time to explore the area.

He soon identified sites that would do nicely for more settlements, with berries and other fruit growing wild, plenty of game, and pastures where cattle could graze. "After a careful examination, we found this place one of the finest on this river," he later wrote.

"I accordingly gave orders to cut down and clear up the woods in the Place Royale, so as to level it and prepare it for building." This clearing ultimately became part of the future city of Montréal.

Champlain was a patient man, but by June 2, he was beginning to wonder if the Huron had chosen not to meet him. He decided to send out Savignon and another man to scout along the river in a canoe that had seen better days, but was the only one available.

They came back a while later saying they hadn't seen any sign of their people.

A Montagnais chief, Outetoucos, said he would go with Savignon for another look, and a young Frenchman named Louis asked if he could tag along. All three set out in the same faulty canoe.

Champlain wasn't worried. Outetoucos and Savignon were both experienced canoeists and wouldn't take any foolish risks.

But when Savignon came back a few days later, he was on foot and alone.

According to him, the three men had gone hunting on an island in the middle of the Lachine Rapids where they had seen a large number of herons. On the way back, they had drifted with the current, but when they hit the rapids, the swirling waters tossed the frail canoe around like a toy until it capsized. Louis, a non-swimmer and dressed in heavy clothing, lost his grip on the sinking craft and was helpless against the power of the current. Outetoucos prided himself on being a strong swimmer, so he set out for the riverbank. He had over-estimated his ability and didn't make it, but Savignon held onto the overturned canoe until it carried him to an eddy near the shore.

Champlain went to see the site for himself the next day and was horrified. "When Savignon showed me the spot, my hair stood on end," he wrote. "There were seven or eight falls where the water goes down by steps, the lowest three feet [one metre] high, and there is an extraordinary seething and boiling." He must have shuddered at how close he had come to losing the young man entrusted to him by Chief Iroquet.

And undoubtedly he would have wondered how his own young man was doing in a country filled with so many potential hazards.

Champlain named the rapids Sault St. Louis after the patron saint of the young man who had died there, and called the body of water above the rapids Lake St. Louis.

Since their only canoe was gone and neither their pinnaces nor their longboats could get past the rapids, the party was at a standstill. They had no choice but to wait for people to arrive. Finally, on June 13,

Ochasteguin and Iroquet appeared with 200 Huron and Algonquin, slowly paddling their canoes in formation toward Place Royale. As they came closer, they began shouting greetings, praising Champlain for having kept his promise.

Champlain went out with Savignon in a canoe to meet them while his men, stationed with muskets on the 13 pinnaces, fired a salute. The explosions were a shock to those who were making their first trip to a trade fair on the St. Lawrence, and they begged the French to stop the awful racket.

Three chiefs, including the brother of Savignon, led the delegation. When they saw the youth they expressed surprised delight, then explained that the Montagnais had told them he was dead. Savignon reassured them that he was fine and had been treated well in France.

As soon as the party landed, friends and family surrounded Savignon and bombarded him with questions, but when he started to tell them all about Paris, they began to doubt either his honesty or his sanity. He spoke of gilded palaces and magnificent gardens where only flowers, no corn or squash, were grown, and tried to describe a strange device for divining what time of day it was. His most outrageous claim was that he had seen the king riding in a golden cabin that rolled along the ground, pulled by eight moose with no antlers.

Champlain grew anxious when he didn't spot Brûlé. The young man was there, but almost unrecognizable in his deerskin breeches, shirt, and moccasins. In order to be accepted by his native hosts, he had made himself as much like them as possible, even shaving off his whiskers, so he wouldn't be the object of teasing and insults. Native peoples found the hairiness of the French rather distasteful.

At length, Brûlé stepped up to his commander and greeted him, probably after having amused himself for several moments by watching Champlain search the faces in the crowd looking for him.

A Shaken Alliance

Pontgravé and the rest of the company traders were at the rendezvous, but once again a horde of free-lancers had shown up as well. Trying to keep a trade fair a secret from them was like trying to keep ants away from spilled molasses.

The traders had brought the most sophisticated goods the Native peoples had ever seen. There were the usual tools and implements, along with shirts, hats, blankets, swords, dried prunes and raisins, hard tack, and vegetable seeds. In the general excitement, brawls broke out, and the Huron chiefs asked Champlain to retire to a quieter spot to sit in on a grand council.

Since Champlain couldn't speak their language, he had to depend on Savignon and Brûlé to help him through a tense meeting.

After the chiefs had thanked Champlain for his kind treatment of Savignon, they moved on to express their concern about seeing so many traders with their shallops and firearms. They said they knew that many of the men were there only for profit and couldn't be counted on as allies. They were willing to see the French come and settle in their country, but only if one man led them, one man alone, one man they could trust. That man was Champlain.

He must have felt like cheering. He had just been handed a perfect argument to present to the regent in favour of a monopoly for his company, and the vote of confidence the Huron had just given him wouldn't do his own career any harm.

But he played the proper diplomat, assuring the chiefs that they didn't have to worry about the traders because all Frenchmen served the king and would honour his alliances.

Temporarily placated, the chiefs presented Champlain with gifts, including four strings of beads, one from each of their four clans, and 50 beaver pelts, one from each of the council headmen.

They said their headmen had sent the furs as a

pledge of their desire to form an alliance with the French. While the headmen couldn't leave their villages all at one time for a trading fair such as this one, they hoped Champlain would go to confer with them in Huronia.

Champlain seized the opportunity to quiz the Huron about their lands, building on the information Brûlé had given him. They answered his questions and even sketched rough maps on the ground, showing distant lakes and rivers and a huge waterfall — the Great Lakes system and Niagara Falls. Champlain was aware that these tribes had developed extensive trading routes far to the west and south, and according to Brûlé, the nations of those distant lands had pelts to trade of the highest quality. This relationship was worth protecting.

The chiefs brought up another problem. They told Champlain that 400 of their men had wanted to come to meet him, but a disturbing rumour had kept them away. Champlain had rescued a Mohawk prisoner the previous year, taking him into French custody, but according to the rumour, Champlain had released him. Then, it was said, he had bribed the Mohawk to arrange for his people to descend on the rendezvous site with 600 warriors and massacre the Huron. The chiefs, of course, didn't believe the rumour. After all, they had come to meet with Champlain, proof enough of their faith in him.

Champlain said firmly that the prisoner had

escaped and he most certainly had not released him, nor was he an ally of the Iroquois League. He had rescued the Mohawk, he added, simply to set an example of how prisoners of war should be treated.

The chiefs seemed to accept his statements, but as the meeting broke up it appeared that their trust was wavering.

The Indispensable Brûlé

Later that night the chiefs again sent for Champlain and Brûlé. Clearly determined to make sure that Champlain understood exactly what they were saying, they asked Brûlé to translate for them. Explaining that they still feared the traders, but still trusted Champlain, they vowed to keep their promise to show him their country, even if it meant risking their lives. They presented him with more pelts and offered to take to their homeland any Frenchman who wanted to go.

Encouraged, Champlain began making promises of his own. He told the chiefs he would ask his king for permission to help them by sending 40 or 50 soldiers for the next year's trading season. The armed force would keep order and drive out the Iroquois once and for all, and the only thing he requested in return was that the Huron would provide food for the soldiers. He would bring priests to teach the Huron about God.

Noticing the approving nods around the council circle, Champlain started to get carried away. He went on to say that settlers would come to live in the region. They would build factories to make the goods the Native peoples coveted. If the lands of Huronia proved fertile, he would establish French settlements there as well, and missions. There was no limit to what their two nations could accomplish together.

Out of the blue the Huron announced they were going beaver hunting. They moved to a site above the rapids where the pinnaces couldn't follow.

Champlain must have asked himself if it was something he had said.

A little while later the chiefs sent for Champlain and the interpreter again.

The two men found that they were guests of honour at an elaborate feast. When it was over, the chiefs called another council where they explained that their beaver-hunting story had been a ruse. They had switched locations because they had heard that the fur traders were going to kill them with their *arquebuses*, and Champlain wouldn't be able to protect them. They asked him not to bring the traders next time.

After countering that he hadn't brought them this time, Champlain vowed to find some way to make sure it wouldn't happen again. And at the time, he meant it.

The Huron reiterated their willingness to help him explore their country and to take some young Frenchmen home with them. Étienne Brûlé would be welcomed by the Bear Clan, and at least two other youths were selected to live with different tribes.

The era of the interpreter had begun. In the years to come, Champlain would send many young men out to live among the Native peoples to gather information that could be obtained only by prolonged residence, not by occasional contact. Brûlé had been the test case, creating the model. Marsolet would become the Montagnais liaison. Others would go out among the many tribes of the Algonquin. All would be the forerunners of the *coureurs-de-bois*, the *voyageurs*, the intrepid adventurers of the future.

A Special Farewell

Before they headed back to their villages, the Huron took care of one more detail, an important one to them. They recovered the body of Outetoucos from the rapids and gave him a secret burial on St. Helen's Island. Then they suggested taking Champlain back to the Montréal settlement site in a canoe.

Champlain knew what that offer meant. If he accepted, he would have to run the rapids. He couldn't swim. He was 44 years old, exhausted from both the physical and mental efforts of the past few days. His experience with canoes was limited, and the memory of the men who had died in the rapids was still fresh in his mind. But he couldn't afford to lose face with the Huron.

Eight canoes made the run, two or three men to each craft. The men stripped themselves naked, but Champlain was allowed to keep a layer of clothing. The Huron told him that if the canoe tipped, he should hold onto it and they would rescue him.

The heart-stopping ride was easy for the Huron. They knew how to rise from their kneeling position to check the waters ahead. They could tell whether waves were harmless or slipping over the top of a submerged boulder. They made adjustments constantly and instinctively, stroking their paddles first on one side of the canoe, then on the other, sometimes dragging them against the current, sometimes going with it.

When he reached a landing after what must have seemed like an eternity, Champlain was soaked and shaken and had acquired new respect for the tough little craft and the expertise of its navigators.

In turn, his bold gesture had won him the admiration of his native allies. His show of raw courage wouldn't have been lost on his protégé, either.

Samuel de Champlain had just set the standard. Now Étienne Brûlé would have to live up to it.

Chapter 6
The People of the Peninsula

I t was four years before Brûlé saw Champlain again. Perhaps the young man travelled to Québec and Tadoussac with fur-trading parties, but again, no one was keeping records that would confirm it. Whether he did or not, he seems to have been left to shift for himself as a guest of the Huron's Bear Clan.

The Huron lived in a relatively small area between Lake Simcoe and the southeast corner of Lake Huron's Georgian Bay. Their territory was bounded on three sides by water, so they called themselves Wendat, sometimes spelled Oendat, meaning People of the Peninsula, or Islanders. Their name for their country was Wendake, or In The Island, though a more poetic version has been suggested, A Land Apart.

The name "Huron" comes from a French word, literally translated as "boar's head," referring to the way the Huron wore their hair in a bristly ridge over the middle of the crown. Alternatively, it means "ruffian" or "lout". In either case, the name doesn't appear to be particularly flattering, but once the French conferred it on them, it refused to go away.

The soil of their homeland was fertile and well farmed by the women, who grew the "three sisters" of native agriculture: squash, corn, and beans. Fish were so abundant it was easy to make a good catch in the lakes and streams, and wild game, though depleted by over-hunting, was still plentiful enough in the forests to supplement their diet.

But it was the multitude of waterways throughout their region that gave the Huron their power. The Huron established trade routes in all directions which linked them to Native peoples throughout the continent.

At various periods, anywhere from 20,000 to 40,000 Huron lived in about 25 villages with populations generally ranging from 200 to 2000, though their largest community, Cahiagué, near present-day Orillia, boasted 6000 residents. Brûlé seems to have spent most of his time living in Touanché, generally considered to be in the vicinity of today's Penetanguishene.

The Huron liked to build their villages at the tops of hills and near an available water supply. They surrounded them with walls made of upright logs sunk into the ground close together and sharpened to a point at the exposed end, forming a circular palisade. Rows of saplings woven through the poles reinforced the barricade, and galleries were added from which they could pour boiling water on attackers.

The towns were close enough together so the people could rush to each other's aid in times of attack or other dangers, and an estimated 330 kilometres of trails linked the villages of the Huron Nation.

Life in the Longhouse

A lodge like the one Étienne Brûlé would have lived in was a windowless longhouse, called *ganonchia* in the Wendat language. On average it could accommodate six families consisting of a woman, her daughters or sisters, their husbands, and their children, who were considered members of their mother's clan.

Constructed by covering an arbour-shaped frame of bent wooden poles with saplings and bark, preferably cedar, a longhouse was typically six to nine metres wide and 25 to 30 metres long, with low doorways at both ends and porches for storing food and firewood.

Openings in the roof let light in and allowed smoke to escape, and could be closed using movable pieces of bark to keep out the elements.

Platforms that lined the walls of the lodge provided workspace during the day and, with the addition of reed mats and animal skins, sleeping areas at night. There were storage areas above and below the platforms for pottery and baskets, weapons and snowshoes, clothes and food. Cooking utensils were hung on cross poles suspended under the ceiling, along with the winter supply of corn braided together by the husks. Strings of squash, dried apples, tobacco, and bundled roots were stored the same way.

Large pieces of bark or reed mats suspended outside the longhouse entryway formed the door, which was secured when everyone was away by wooden bars, but only to keep out the dogs. Anyone who had valuables to protect buried them in secret places. The thickness of the door was doubled in winter to keep in as much heat as possible, but in extremely frigid weather it became necessary to pile on extra clothes and furs.

Painted above the door was the symbol of the clan who lived there. Brûlé's clan was the Attignawantan, the People of the Bear. The other clans were the Deer People, the Rock People, and the Barking Dogs.

To the priests who arrived a few years later from

Étienne Brûlé

their quiet, immaculate seminaries in France, these living conditions were shocking. Not only was there an utter lack of privacy, the smoky longhouses were overrun with seemingly undisciplined children, dogs that snatched at the food the Huron shared with them, and mice, rats, fleas, and lice. On hot days, the smell of drying fish mingled unpleasantly with tobacco, sweat, and garbage odours, and sanitation facilities were minimal to non-existent.

When the village became too over-run with waste and the farmland had lost its fertility, the people simply picked up and moved on to a new site to start fresh. They even transported the residents of their cemeteries, too venerated to be left alone and unguarded.

Brûlé, who had been brought up in rustic surroundings, apparently had no problem adjusting to life in a longhouse, and the chiefs who had worried he might become ill from a change in diet needn't have been concerned. It is doubtful he had ever eaten so well in his life, or so nutritiously. Meals were varied, the portions generous. His hosts were hospitable people who regularly held feasts and celebrations with lots of singing, dancing, contests, games, and theatrical ceremonies. Illness might call for a Curing Feast, imminent death for a Farewell Feast, a run of especially good fortune a Thanksgiving Feast. And when they moved their villages and cemeteries, there was the most important festival of all, the Feast of the Dead.

The Bravest of the Brave

Brûlé's companions taught him to spear fish in the streams and gather a good catch even in winter by dropping a line and hook through a hole in the ice that covered the lakes and rivers. Whitefish, trout, pike, sturgeon — the variety seemed never-ending.

Brûlé learned to play hockey, or at least its Huron forerunner, a fast-moving game involving curved sticks and a wooden ball, played on a field of snow.

He would have joined a lacrosse team and played in the wild free-for-all that was as much battle training as sport. Up to 100 players joined together to make up each team, and the game was played over wide areas with goals sometimes a few kilometres apart. A game could last for days and leave a trail of injuries, even deaths.

As a newcomer, Brûlé would have faced challenges designed to test his mettle, from entering races against the fastest runners of the village to taking part in endurance contests. In one such test, he would tie his forearm to the arm of a Huron man. Then both men would place their lashed-together arms on a piece of lighted tinder and try to hold them there without flinching until the tinder had burned itself out. The first man to pull back was judged to be lacking in courage, the most highly prized virtue.

He joined war parties and learned to ambush small groups of Iroquois. He assisted at torture rituals, and if he didn't develop a taste for the practice, he definitely became hardened to it.

Huron men loved to gamble, playing their own version of dice, and it wouldn't have taken young Brûlé long to pick up the habit.

The Huron, natural orators and storytellers, admired Brûlé's ability to speak to them in their own language. The young ladies appreciated it, too. It has been suggested, only somewhat jokingly, that one of the main reasons Brûlé was so eager to learn the native languages was that he wanted to be able to talk to the pretty girls. By most accounts, he was an incorrigible womanizer throughout the years he spent with the Huron, and their relaxed attitudes toward the dalliances of their young people gave him plenty of opportunity to indulge himself.

According to the writings of Champlain and the priests who eventually set up missions around Georgian Bay, young Huron men and women were free to choose and discard partners at will, living together without feeling compelled to marry, and enjoying romantic adventures without fear of reproach. Even if they did decide to wed, then come to regret it, they could divorce easily, though if a couple had children they usually stayed together. If they didn't, the whole clan took responsibility for their young.

Champlain recorded that quite often "a woman spent her youth in this fashion, having had more than a dozen or fifteen husbands, all of whom were not the only men to enjoy the woman. After nightfall the young women and girls run about from one lodge to another, as do the young men for their part on the same quest, possessing them whenever it seems good, yet without any violence, leaving all to the wishes of the women .... and no shame, disgrace or dishonour being incurred." He insisted he himself had been forced to rebuff more than a few propositions.

Perhaps Champlain's claims should be taken with a grain of salt. Huron women worked hard cultivating their crops, making and decorating clothing, weaving baskets, preparing food both for immediate meals and for the winter larder. Literally, as well as figuratively, they kept the home fires burning, so it is hard to believe they had the time or energy for such strenuous socializing.

Champlain, like the missionaries who followed him into Huron country, had good reason to suggest in the reports back to France that the Native peoples were

Étienne Brûlé

godless and lacked any moral sense. Extra resources might be shaken loose for the sake of bringing them into the Christian fold and teaching them to behave the way Europeans thought they should behave. What was a little embellishment if it furthered his cause?

Whatever the precise truth might be, there was enough of a relaxed moral attitude to appeal to a lusty young Frenchman. By the time there were priests to be witness to his many sins — yet somehow not to his many achievements — Brûlé was said to have taken and discarded more than his share of mistresses and fathered numerous children, and the missionaries had little to say about him that was good. Récollet brother Gabriel Sagard described Brûlé as "very vicious in character and much addicted to women," and a Jesuit complained that he was a stumbling block to the conversion of the Huron because of his "shocking way of life." Others called him "an infamous wretch," and said he was "guilty of every vice and crime."

Brûlé had been instructed to learn about native customs, not to adopt them himself. He was supposed to influence the Huron, not emulate them.

Brûlé, for his part, continued to wear the Lamb of God medal he still had from his childhood, suspended from a chain looped around his neck.

A Run of Bad Luck

While Étienne Brûlé was in the wilds of Canada trans-forming himself from a French farm boy into an interpreter, an emissary, and a sometime warrior of the Bear Clan, Champlain was wheeling and dealing, trying desperately to keep the whole endeavour from falling apart.

Champlain left for France in mid-August that summer of 1611 and arrived on September 10 to find that his backers wanted out. The fur trade profits had been too skimpy to warrant further participation. He decided to try once more for a monopoly, but on the way to Paris he fell off his horse and was laid up just long enough to give competing fur merchants time to get to the royal palace first.

Champlain spent more than a year trying to retrench. As a result he didn't get back to Québec the next summer.

The Algonquin and Huron, waiting at Lachine for the commander and soldiers who never arrived, were less than pleased.

He immersed himself in writing his journals, which kept him busy until he received good news in October, 1612. There was a new Viceroy of New France, Prince Charles de Bourbon, and he was enthusiastic about the Québec colony. The Prince had obtained a Royal

Commission for a 12-year monopoly in the fur trade and Champlain was to be his agent with the title, for the first time, of Lieutenant.

Finally, something was going right.

Then Charles de Bourbon died of smallpox. His authority was transferred to Henri de Bourbon, Prince de Condé, who became Viceroy of New France in the fall of 1612 and who expressed a desire to keep Champlain on as Lieutenant. Champlain was authorized to restructure a broad corporation to include merchants from Rouen and La Rochelle, his former competitors. Instead of sabotaging his colonizing efforts, perhaps they would have a vested interest in seeing the settlement succeed.

The Lure of the Salt Sea
Champlain returned to New France in the spring of 1613, fired up by a special mission. He was going to head up the Ottawa River to see if it would take him to the great salt sea of the north, whether the Montagnais and Algonquin would lead the way or not.

He had a guide of his own, a young man named Nicolas de Vignau. De Vignau had spent several months in an Algonquin village on an island in the Ottawa River and was insisting he had been to the body of water later known as Hudson Bay, led there by the Nipissing tribe. He claimed it could be reached in just seventeen days from Lachine, and he offered details that matched reports of the mutiny of Henry Hudson's crew, as evidence of what he had seen.

Champlain had decided to check out the story himself. If de Vignau was right, a northern passage to the Orient could be within reach.

When he arrived in Tadoussac he found the Montagnais on the verge of starvation, so desperate they had been reduced to eating entrails and the tallow used for caulking the ship.

He also found renegade traders defying his monopoly, and this time they were Frenchmen, not Spanish Basques. He later learned that the illustrious new Viceroy had been engaged in a complicated game of double-dealing and separate contract negotiations with the La Rochelle merchants, thus undermining Champlain's newly structured company.

At the moment, though, all Champlain knew was that he had to cope with illicit traders yet again. However, he was more concerned about his settlement, so he headed to Québec. To his relief he found that it had weathered another winter quite comfortably.

He pushed on to Lachine, expecting his Huron and Algonquin allies to be there to greet him. When he got there he found only a few Algonquin travelling down the river with furs. They told him the free traders had treated the Native peoples badly the previous year and the tribes had decided not to come back. Champlain's long absence had convinced them he would never return, and some of the traders had spread the story that he was dead. Deciding they couldn't expect any more help from the French, a large party of Huron and Algonquin had gone on the warpath against the Iroquois on their own.

Champlain had brought only five men with him on this expedition, not enough to make up for the broken promises of the past. But he figured he could make an effort to reconnect with the Algonquin up the Ottawa River while he was verifying de Vignau's story.

What he didn't realize was that he was about to imperil an already damaged alliance and come close to undoing all of Étienne Brûlé's hard work.

A New Riddle

Champlain retraced the journey Étienne Brûlé had made on his way to Huronia two years before, but with a significant difference. Brûlé had travelled with a large contingent of Algonquin and Huron warriors. Champlain's guides consisted of Nicolas de Vignau and one native man, the only members of the party with canoeing experience.

Travelling in two canoes, they set out for the

Ottawa. The journey was difficult. At one point, Champlain nearly lost a hand when his craft crashed into a rock. Meeting a party of Algonquin, he managed to persuade them to provide guides who showed them a detour around a rapid-torn section.

They made their way through a number of small lakes, portaging between them. At times they had to drag the heavily loaded canoes while walking along the riverbanks or wading through the water, plagued by insects. Portaging under the weight of their canoes and paddles, plus their muskets, heavy clothes, and various essentials, they had to fight their way through the wilderness.

Along the way, it seems Champlain lost a navigational device that wasn't found until 1867. Champlain's Astrolabe is the most famous artifact of New France.

Another Setback

The long struggle ended at the Algonquin village on Allumette Island where de Vignau had lived, opposite present-day Pembroke, Ontario.

The village chief greeted Champlain with apparent pleasure and ordered a feast, but the pleasantries gradually turned into mutual acrimony.

Champlain suggested that the chief had been using pretexts to block French efforts to explore the north, and to keep them from making contact with the Nipissing. The Algonquin, Champlain said, had called the Nipissing sorcerers and claimed they were hostile, yet de Vignau had met them and said those charges were false. Furthermore, de Vignau had seen the great salt sea.

The chief shot back that de Vignau was lying about having been to the salt sea and had never left the village or met the Nipissing, who most certainly were evil sorcerers. He made such dire threats against de Vignau that the terrified youth broke down and threw himself on Champlain's mercy, admitting he had made up the whole thing.

It took some doing to patch things up with the Algonquin and persuade them to accompany him to Lachine for some trading, but Champlain managed it. Then he suggested sending another youth to live with the Algonquin, and the chief refused. He said he didn't care to play host to young men who told lies about him and his people.

Before the chief gave in, Champlain had to do a lot of fast talking. He was furious about the embarrassment and the unnecessary tension, not to mention the time he had lost by listening to de Vignau's lies.

At Lachine, de Vignau made his formal confession, saying he had invented the tale in the hope of getting a reward, never dreaming Champlain would investigate the facts personally.

Champlain pardoned the young man, and de Vignau disappears from the records, possibly killed by the Algonquin. In later years, Champlain still wondered if the youth's real lie was his original story or his confession.

Chapter 7
The First Missionaries

Champlain went back to France in the autumn of 1613, where he struggled to keep the financing for his colonial efforts on track. He missed another trading season in 1614, another opportunity to support his native allies against the Iroquois, another chance to stay one step ahead of rival explorers from England and Holland.

His critics were saying that his outposts in New France were few, small, and vulnerable. His alliance with the Algonquin and Huron had become shaky. And the promise he had made to the Native peoples to establish another settlement at Place Royale on Montréal Island didn't hold much appeal for investors. They were tired of paying for colonies that didn't turn a profit.

By 1613, the English had established a thriving colony in Virginia that was producing tobacco, a lucrative cash crop. The Dutch had staked discovery claims along the Hudson River and were ready to venture into Iroquois country to trade furs. Meanwhile, the French had lost Acadia, the east coast region stretching from Cape Cod to the Bay of Fundy, to the English.

It was time for a new strategy. Champlain created "The Company of Canada," and as he travelled through France gathering support for his corporation and his cause. He began to shift the emphasis away from the fur trade and towards spreading Christianity and the French language and culture to the Native peoples. One of his contacts suggested that the members of the Récollet order might be willing to go to New France.

The Récollets were an austere Franciscan order devoted to charitable works and tending the sick. Since they had already established missions in Spanish America, they had some experience in the New World, and since part of their creed was to embrace poverty they expected to adapt easily to whatever desperate conditions they might find.

Funds were raised to finance the efforts of four Récollet missionaries, and they left France with Champlain on April 24, 1615, eager to make their way to the Nipissing and Huron lands.

They reached Québec in mid-May. One of the priests, Father Le Caron, wanted to proceed to Huronia right away. Champlain suggested he might prefer to spend the winter in Québec and head out in the spring, but Le Caron was insistent.

The party journeyed to Lachine for the annual meeting with the Algonquin and Huron, but few Native people turned up and those who did were wary. Étienne Brûlé was there with his Huron companions, now fully conversant in their language and usually referred to as "the interpreter."

It is difficult to say what he thought when he first saw the priests, but it wouldn't be long before he would be wishing he had never laid eyes on them.

A Crucial Decision

With Étienne Brûlé's help, Champlain and the Native people parleyed, and agreed to use the Huron village of Cahiagué as the jumping-off point for a major offensive against the Iroquois.

Champlain said he would supply as many men as he could muster, and the Huron promised 2500 warriors. They wanted Champlain to go with them at once to their country, but he said he had to head back to Québec to make preparations for such an important expedition, and would be back in four or five days. He left for the settlement, taking Brûlé with him.

Champlain's four or five days turned into ten, and with the trade activities completed, the Huron wanted to go home.

As the days passed, they started to worry that the Iroquois, who weren't far away, might have killed Champlain. Father Le Caron was pushing to leave, eager to begin his mission work. Finally, he started out with a large group of native men and 12 Frenchmen. Only four or five of them knew how to handle firearms, and those not very well.

At Québec, Champlain was having trouble getting up a party to go with him. One canoe left, followed a week later by another with a handful of Huron, a personal servant, and Brûlé. Between the two parties, 16 Frenchmen were headed into Huron country. It wasn't the promised 40 or 50, but it was the largest number to date.

The going was hard. Meals consisted of *sagamité*, a corn meal mush with game or fish added to it. The meat was rarely washed, the fish rarely gutted, the cooking kettles rarely cleaned, according to Champlain.

He did enjoy the blueberries and raspberries he found along the way.

After a long, strenuous trip involving many

portages, Champlain's party reached Georgian Bay. He cupped his hand and dipped it into the water, tasted it, and called the bay, *La Mer Douce*, the Sweetwater Sea.

Three weeks after they had started out, Champlain and his companions reached Touanché, the village of the Bear Clan. They had covered 1125 arduous kilometres in 23 days.

It was here that Champlain experienced the flirtation he wrote about later: "A shameless girl came boldly up to me, offering to keep me company, which I declined with thanks, sending her away with gentle remonstrances." He had gone outside the longhouse where he was staying, hoping to escape the fleas, but the girl obviously assumed he was looking for a pleasant interlude in the cornfield. She must have been baffled when he turned her down and gave her a prim scolding.

Brûlé acted as Champlain's guide as they toured the Huron villages. Champlain was keen to fulfill his commitment to battle the Iroquois. The Huron were assembling a large war party, but they were moving slowly. Champlain went from village to village to urge the chiefs to gather at Cahiagué. The selected battle site was an Iroquois settlement, possibly in today's upstate New York, near Syracuse. Some sources say the target was the Mohawk, others favour the Oneida or the Onondaga. Champlain's accounts aren't helpful, since

Paddling the waters of Georgian Bay c. 1615. Champlain
(probably with Étienne Brûlé) is scouting the way.

he never got the clan structures straight for either the
Huron or the Iroquois.

Of the 2500 warriors he had been promised, at best
count there were perhaps 500 gathered in Cahiagué by
August 17.

Then, important news arrived. The Susquehannock,
also called Carantouans or Andastes, a maverick group
of Iroquoian descent who lived on the banks of the

Susquehanna River in what is now eastern Pennsylvania, wanted to join the attack with 500 warriors.

Champlain and the Huron were delighted. They could trap the Iroquois between the Huron attack from the north and the Susquehannock offensive from the south.

But someone would have to take word to the new allies and lead them to the battle site. A dozen of the best warriors were selected for the mission.

Brûlé requested permission to go with them.

Knowing he could count on Brûlé to bring back detailed and accurate information about the country south of the great inland lakes, Champlain agreed readily in spite of the dangers he knew the young man would face.

Brûlé was fully aware of the risks. After four years with the Huron, he was far from the wide-eyed innocent he had been when he had first arrived in New France. He understood perfectly the implications of heading into the heart of Iroquois territory, through country he had never seen, to meet with an unfamiliar tribe. If he got that far, he would have to gather the warriors and lead them to the battle site. At every step of the way he would be in danger of being captured, tortured, and killed.

How could he resist?

The First Missionaries

Preparing for Battle

It took another two weeks for both the attack party and Brûlé's crew to leave Cahiagué. A principal chief of the Rock Clan, Atironta, was part of the expedition, along with Chief Iroquet and his men, and other Algonquin who had wintered with the Huron. Every group that arrived was welcomed with feasts and dancing.

Champlain grew impatient as he saw autumn approaching with no real progress.

Finally, on September 1, he and his force of armed Frenchmen and warriors started out, moving eastward to the narrows between Lakes Couchiching and Simcoe at present-day Orillia. They paused there for another week of preparations and to wait for stragglers from other parts of Huronia to join them.

It was September 8 before Brûlé and the 12 Huron warriors could leave on their mission. The date set for the attack was October 11. Champlain would expect Brûlé to be at the battle site on the eve of October 10 with the promised reinforcements from the Susquehannock.

Brûlé and his companions crossed Lake Simcoe and went up the Holland River as far as they could go, then shouldered their canoes and portaged to the Humber River. They followed it to its mouth at Lake Ontario, where the city of Toronto now stands.

Their route from this point is unclear, since

Champlain's second-hand account isn't specific. He wrote only that the party tried to avoid an encounter with the Iroquois by sticking to dense forests, thickets, and marshy swamps. In spite of their caution, they met up with a band of hostile Iroquois, but killed four of them and took two prisoners to be tortured at Carantouan, the Susquehannock capital.

When they reached Carantouan, the Susquehannock celebrated with several days and nights of feasting, intensifying the war fever, but wasting precious time. Although Brûlé tried to prod them, his urgings had little effect. A grand council was called to decide whether the 500 warriors should be sent, which must have exasperated Brûlé after they had initiated the plan in the first place and he had risked his life to get to them.

The decision was favourable, but more delays followed, and Brûlé's chances of making his deadline were growing slimmer by the day.

Champlain's Humiliation
Champlain's party made its way through the beautiful Kawartha Lakes and Trent River country, savouring a late-summer interlude in what would become popular cottage country in a future century.

They emerged at today's Bay of Quinte on Lake Ontario, then proceeded to the eastern end of the lake, crossed to the south side of the St. Lawrence, and hid their canoes in the forest. They pushed west on foot, moving quietly. Champlain's plan called for a surprise attack, theoretically synchronized with the Susquehannock thrust from the south.

In early October they stopped near the target Iroquois village and built a fortified war camp, where they stayed for the next 10 days.

Champlain planned to keep the presence of the French a secret as long as possible, but his allies were eager to get started and were increasingly difficult to control. He was still operating on the European line-of-command model, while the Huron listened to his lectures with little more than mild interest. Their attitude was that he had as much right to speak his mind as anyone, but unless he convinced them he was right they felt no obligation to obey his orders.

On the afternoon of October 11 — a day late for the rendezvous with Brûlé — the allied war party saw the Iroquois working in their cornfields outside the village fortification. The Huron screamed and rushed to the attack, and Champlain was helpless to hold them back. The Iroquois drove them off, wounding several. Champlain and his Frenchmen used their muskets to force the Iroquois to retreat, but all hope of surprising the enemy had been lost.

Champlain laced into the Huron warriors, who had been chastened enough to decide they should listen to him. Under his direction, they built a medieval cavalier, a moveable wooden tower high enough to overlook the palisade and large enough to hold four or five marksmen. He also had thick wooden screens made, called mantelets, to protect the attackers as they advanced on the Iroquois fort to set fire to it.

The Iroquois fortress was impressive, consisting of four palisades with double-timbered galleries that provided a defence against musket fire. It was near a pond so the Iroquois had access to water to put out fires.

Once again, the Native people and Champlain were at odds, but this time they wanted to hold back and he was in a hurry to attack. They felt they should wait for the Susquehannock. Champlain believed they were strong enough to take the village on their own. His opinion prevailed.

Some 200 warriors carried the tower to within a metre of the stockade and set it in place. Three French soldiers mounted it with their muskets and opened fire on the Iroquois along the galleries who had been hurling rocks and shooting arrows at the Huron.

The Huron abandoned the mantelets and rushed out into the open, yelling insults and shooting arrows into the fort, where the defenders easily dodged them.

The attackers set fires in the wrong places, so the wind blew the flames away from the palisade.

Champlain bellowed out orders, but there was too much noise. Besides, he wasn't speaking their language. Even if they had heard him, they wouldn't have known what he was saying.

He had never needed Étienne Brûlé more, but Brûlé and the Susquehannock were nowhere to be seen.

The only thing left for Champlain to do was have his Frenchmen shoot all the Iroquois they could see.

The attack lasted three hours and ended with the Huron running from a storm of arrows. Two chiefs were wounded, and Champlain was hit in the leg and knee. It was a rout.

He wrote later that when they were back in their fortification he upbraided the native warriors and pleaded for a renewed attack, but they agreed only to wait a few days longer for the Susquehannock and then try again. After four days of hit-and-run attacks by the Iroquois, who called them cowards for needing the French to fight their battles, the Huron and their allies decided to retreat.

They bound their wounded in a crouching position and carried them in basket-weave litters on their backs, placing them at the centre of the party while well-armed men surrounded them.

Champlain, one of the wounded, admired the orderly withdrawal, but found it an excruciating experience. "Never did I find myself in such a hell as during this time," he wrote. "For the pain I suffered from the wound in my knee was nothing in comparison with what I endured tied and bound on the back of one of our savages. This made me lose patience, and as soon as I gained strength to stand, I got out of that prison."

When the retreating war party reached their canoes, Champlain told the Huron he wanted to go back to Montréal and Québec by way of the St. Lawrence. If they didn't want to guide him, they could give him a canoe so he and some of his Frenchmen could find their own way.

The native men refused, saying he would either drown in the rapids or be captured by the Iroquois. They insisted he would have to go to Québec by way of the standard circle route: first back to Huronia, then on through the waterways to the Ottawa River.

Champlain was about to spend a winter with the Huron whether he liked it or not, and when it was over, he would never venture into the interior again. After this experience, his exploring days would be over.

Brûlé's Miraculous Escape

Brûlé arrived at the Iroquois village two days after the

war party had left and saw the evidence of what had happened. The village seemed relatively unaffected by the attack, but there was no way to judge the extent of the damage to the allies.

Winter was moving in, and to get back to Huronia would involve another trek through the country of the angered Iroquois.

Brûlé went back to Carantouan while his Huron warriors apparently struck out for home.

Over the winter he travelled with the Susquehannock, probably on their trading expeditions. He followed the Susquehanna River all the way to Chesapeake Bay, and reported later to Champlain that he had learned of powerful nations who lived on the riverbanks and were constantly at war with each other. When he reached the ocean he explored nearby coastal areas, where the Native peoples told him the Dutch traders had been treating them badly. They had nothing against the French, however. He reported that the climate was mild, with hardly any snow, and game was plentiful.

He had covered much of the huge area now known as eastern Pennsylvania, never before seen by any European. Captain John Smith had explored the bay in 1608 for the English, but hadn't travelled more than three kilometres upriver.

Brûlé returned to Carantouan in the spring, and

the Susquehannock offered him six warriors as an escort back to Huron country. When the party ran into a band of Iroquois in Seneca country, the warriors scattered and Brûlé ran for his life. Soon he was hopelessly lost in the forest.

He had been wandering for several days when he happened upon three Iroquois, probably Seneca, who had been fishing and were on their way back to their village.

He decided to take a chance and approach them. At first they were frightened, but he talked to them in the Huron language, put down his weapons, and asked them to do the same. They did, then led him back to their village and offered him something to eat. Afterwards, they took him to the longhouse of their principal headmen or chiefs, who questioned him. Brûlé tried to say he wasn't a Frenchman, but they didn't believe him. Warriors tied him to a torture post in the middle of their village and subjected him to the ghastly rituals he had witnessed, and probably participated in, so many times.

According to the story Brûlé later told Champlain and others, he was sure he was doomed until suddenly God stepped in and saved him. When one of his tormentors made a grab for the Lamb of God medal he was wearing, Brûlé reacted angrily. "If you touch that," he shouted, "you and all your race will die." He pointed to the dark clouds and claimed they were signs of God's anger.

The storm broke. Jagged spears of lightning and booming explosions of thunder frightened the Native people out of their wits. They ran away, leaving Brûlé tied to the tree. He tried to cajole them into coming out and untying him, but it was only after a long while that one of the headmen ventured out, set him free, led him to his own lodge, and dressed his wounds.

When the storm ended and Brûlé had recovered enough to speak to the tribe, he called a meeting of the village and delivered an eloquent speech. The French were "next of kin to the angels," he said, obviously having decided to admit he was French. The Dutch, on the other hand, were "the bad manitous or spirits." He promised to make the Iroquois friends with the French, and said he would return to them as soon as he could to seal this new alliance.

From then on he was treated as the tribe's honoured guest and invited to their feasts and celebrations. When it was time for him to go back to Huronia, they sent several men to guide him part of the way.

There are a few problems with Brûlé's story. Certainly he was tortured, and obviously he escaped with his life. But his later claim of divine intervention doesn't ring true. In the account of Brother Gabriel Sagard, the rascal Brûlé added a detail that sounds suspiciously like he was teasing the priest just for the fun of it. "He did not know to which saint he could give himself, " Sagard wrote, referring to Brûlé. "He was not devout, judging by what he told us. He said to us one day that, finding himself in another great peril of death, for prayer he said his Bénédicité."

A Bénédicité is grace before a meal, hardly the kind of prayer even a lapsed Catholic would offer up at such a time.

A more likely version is that the Iroquois headmen talked the situation over, figured they could use this Huron-speaking Frenchman to their advantage, and stopped the torture. They were having problems with the Dutch traders. An alliance with the French probably seemed like a good idea.

Brûlé may have promised to make peace between the French and the Iroquois just to keep them happy until he got safely away. Then again, it is possible he meant every word and maintained contact with them from that time on. He was the fur-trading equivalent of the travelling salesman, and it was his job to find new partners to trade with. He had just identified a prospect.

But whatever yarns he was spinning for the priests and any other audiences he could muster when he got back to Huronia, he still had to face Champlain.

A Tense Reunion

Brûlé stayed put for a while, though in his case "staying put" meant restricting his explorations to minor trips around the shores of Lake Huron.

In the spring of 1618 he went down to the Three Rivers trade fair, where he and Champlain met for the first time since they had parted ways in Cahiagué, Champlain to head for the battle site, Brûlé to collect the Susquehannock.

Still smarting from his humiliating defeat and his enforced sojourn in Huronia, Champlain demanded an explanation. Why hadn't Brûlé shown up with reinforcements? Where the devil had he been all this time? Why hadn't he made any reports?

Brûlé told his sad tale, complete with pious embellishments, and showed the commander some of the scars he had earned at the torture post.

Champlain's anger dissipated in a cloud of sympathy and remorse. Later, he wrote of Brûlé, "He is more to be pitied than blamed for not reporting to me before, because of the misfortunes he experienced on his journeys."

However, business was business, and there was no sense dwelling on the past. Champlain briskly instructed Brûlé to continue his work and undertake new explorations, for which he would be given extra rewards. Champlain also told Brûlé to pass on the word to the Huron that he would return the following year with more fighting men to help them in their wars.

He still hoped to establish a base in Huronia for exploration to the west. He had heard stories from the Native peoples of a large island in Lake Huron and rapids at the end of the lake, beyond which was a body of water so large that the other side of it couldn't be seen from its shores. Check it out, he ordered.

So Brûlé checked it out, but not right away.

Five more years passed before Brûlé set out on a major journey of exploration. During those years he meandered through the many islands and inlets of Georgian Bay and met with the various native groups of the area, still promoting his company's business, still Champlain's main man in the interior. Champlain seemed to forget all about the reward he had promised Brûlé, and never showed up with the fighting force for the Huron, but no one seemed to hold it against him, least of all Brûlé.

Some time between 1621 and 1623, Brûlé teamed up with another interpreter named Grenolle and headed out at last to search for the long-reported western sea. Their assignment was to try to bring about peace among the warring native groups of the area and urge the western tribes to take their furs to the great trading fairs at Montréal. In addition, Champlain was still intrigued by the strip of copper the Algonquin had given him all those years ago, so his instructions to Brûlé had included a search for copper mines.

The two explorers paddled along the north shore of Georgian Bay, possibly with a party of Huron, though the records make no mention of native guides. Eventually they entered the waterway between the rugged mainland and a long chain of large and small islands, now called the North Channel. They found Native peoples who mined copper, and Brûlé collected a large ingot to take back with him as evidence.

Pushing on, they reached the rapids of what is now St. Mary's River, though Gabriel Sagard's account of the voyage refers to the rapids as Sault de Gaston. They had reached the outlet of Lake Superior, which Champlain later called Grand Lac, and the hub of some of the continent's principal waterways, opening up the route to enormous territories.

Once and for all they could report that this great inland sea was a freshwater lake, not connected directly to Hudson Bay.

The Native people living by the rapids told Brûlé and Grenolle of still more lakes to the north and west, but said they were deathly afraid of the people who lived there.

It is believed that the explorers continued along the north shore of Lake Superior to the farthest end of the lake, where the city of Duluth now stands, but no one knows for certain. If either of them wrote an account of their incredible journey, it has disappeared.

Only the journal of the Récollet Brother Sagard, who arrived in Huronia in 1623 and heard the details from Brûlé himself, stands as testimony that the first Europeans to set eyes on the world's largest freshwater lake were a couple of unkempt rogues paddling a paper-thin canoe.

The Saint and the Sinner
What bothered Brother Gabriel Sagard about Étienne Brûlé was that the interpreter was supposed to be converting the Native peoples, but it looked as if they had converted him.

Sagard and Brûlé first met in Québec in the spring of 1623. Brûlé was there for the commercial season and to make his report to Champlain. Sagard had arrived from France to carry on the work of the Récollets.

At this point in his career, Brûlé was paid directly by the fur merchants to represent them with the local traders, as were several other interpreters. Brûlé was the highest paid of the lot, receiving 100 *pistoles* to act as their representative. For a young man who had nowhere to spend his money except during the few weeks of the trade fairs, it was a generous salary, but Brûlé didn't seem to be interested in material success. If he had been, he could have used his skills and connections to make his fortune in the fur trade. More and more, it appears that he did what he did strictly for the love of it.

The commercial and military alliance between the French and the Native peoples had started to worry Champlain. The intrigues and shifting alliances in the New World were becoming as unsettling and unpredictable as those of the Old.

A rumour was going around that the Huron wanted to make peace with the Iroquois in order to start trading with the Dutch, whose trading posts were now closer and more accessible than those of the French, and whose goods were cheaper.

The cultural exchanges that had continued over the years had opened the eyes of the young native men visiting France to the actual worth of some of the goods their people had been buying, and they'd returned home to report that the French had been swindling them.

The situation called for a renewal of the relationship with France's native allies, so Champlain decided to send a delegation to spend the winter with the Huron and encourage the native men to return with them to Québec in the spring to forge a new treaty.

Three Récollets, including Gabriel Sagard, and six other Frenchmen accompanied Brûlé to Huronia.

Brûlé and Sagard lived in different villages in Huronia, and Sagard was there for only a year, but they got together often enough to drive each other to distraction.

Sagard was shocked by Brûlé's adoption of native ways, especially his sexual morality, or more precisely, what Sagard considered his lack of sexual morality. As far as Sagard was concerned, the continued presence of Brûlé and the rest of the interpreters and fur traders among the Native peoples would keep the latter mired in their traditional practices and remove whatever chance they had of salvation.

Offended, and not at all impressed by the condescending attitudes of their countrymen, the interpreters launched a protest by refusing to teach the missionaries the native languages.

Brûlé must have softened on that score, because it is generally accepted that the Huron–English dictionary Sagard compiled could not have been accomplished without Brûlé's help in the short time the missionary was in Huronia.

Brûlé spent the winter as he usually did, hunting

and ice-fishing, touring the countryside, playing sports, and chasing women.

The priests worked at learning the language and observing native customs, and said the mass every Sunday, assisted by some of the Frenchmen and a few curious Huron.

Friendly Extortion
When spring arrived, Brûlé set off for Québec, accompanied by about 200 Huron men, their canoes loaded with furs.

Sagard headed out from his village to catch up with them, telling the other priests at the mission that he would be back as soon as possible. They travelled as fast as they could and caught up with Brûlé's party at an island village of the Algonquin.

The chief had a feast set out consisting of a huge sturgeon boiled in a broth with corn meal stirred into it. Food was more scarce the rest of the way, and included such dubious delicacies as eagle and a stray dog, the head presented with great pride to Sagard. He couldn't bring himself to eat it, and exchanged the choice morsel for a leg.

For some of the trip, Sagard and Brûlé shared a canoe, which gave Brûlé plenty of opportunity to tease the missionary, who seems to have been easy to bait. At one point the native canoeists pointed out a large rock that looked like a human head with two upraised arms. They said it had been a man, but he had been turned to stone. They made a tobacco offering to the man-like rock to ensure the success of their journey.

When Sagard expressed his shock at this evidence of blatant idolatry, Brûlé casually mentioned that he had taken part in the ceremony himself once, and the season had been his most profitable ever.

Sagard huffed that such superstitions were the work of the devil.

Brûlé probably threw back his head and roared with laughter, having goaded the strait-laced priest to anger once again.

But there were moments when Sagard was grateful for the expertise of his companions. In his account of the journey, he admits he was glad to have Brûlé with him in times of danger, admired his courage and endurance, and was impressed by how Brûlé could paddle long distances without seeming to tire.

Yet when they reached Québec and Sagard reported to Champlain, he criticized the way most of the interpreters and French fur traders lived, saying they had become "more savage than the savages."

Champlain listened to the priest's complaints, becoming increasingly angry at the unseemly behaviour of these unruly men who were a disgrace to France. He seemed particularly disappointed with Brûlé.

Whatever shreds of friendship the man and his protégé still had seems to have ended with Sagard's report.

Chapter 8
Brûlé's Star Fades

rom this point on, Brûlé all but disappears from view, as if he had ceased to exist. Even Champlain's maps of the period reflect none of the geographical information he was receiving from Brûlé and his colleagues.

But we catch glimpses of him now and then.

We see him in Québec for the trading season in 1625. Champlain is in France and Émery de Caën is in charge of the colony.

Reportedly a despot, de Caën appears to have been disliked by the settlers. One of the inhabitants was Louis Hébert, generally recognized as Canada's first French farmer. Hébert had been with Champlain since the old days at Port Royal in Acadia, so perhaps he was singled out by de Caën to be put in his place. Whatever the reason, the two men were at odds. Under financial pressure, Hébert needed a loan, and Étienne Brûlé offered to give him whatever he needed to tide him over at no interest.

De Caën heard about the transaction and was enraged. He refused to allow this lowly interpreter to meddle in the financial affairs of the colony. He would make the loan himself — at 25 percent interest.

It must have been with a snort of disgust that Brûlé headed back into the wilderness.

The next time we see Brûlé, it is in a priest's journal, mentioning the missionary's travels to the country of the Neutral, "of which the interpreter Brûlé told wonders."

No one knows what the Neutral called themselves. The name the French gave them comes from the fact that they refused to involve themselves in the wars of their neighbours. It was probably a sensible decision. They lived in about 40 villages on the shores of Lake Erie, along a belt that stretches between the present-day Niagara and Detroit Rivers, directly between their sister nations of the Iroquois League and the Huron Confederacy. Not only did the Neutral deem it wise not to take sides, they made weapons and tools, which they sold to both the Huron and the Iroquois.

Brûlé probably first saw the Neutral at some point during his trek in 1615 to the Susquehannock territory, and seems to have spent two winters visiting them, roughly around 1625.

By this time, Brûlé had seen at least four of the five Great Lakes, most likely all five. It has been suggested that he missed Lake Michigan, possibly having assumed it was just another section of Lake Huron. But it seems unlikely that when he was on St. Mary's River, and had talked at length with the Native people there about the area, that he would have committed such an oversight.

The Jesuits
The year 1625 saw another pivotal development in the unfolding story of New France: the arrival of the Jesuit priests, Fathers Massé, Lalement, and de Brébeuf.

The Récollets claimed that, lacking the resources to do justice to the work needed in Huronia, they had invited the Jesuits to join them. But in fact the latest Viceroy of New France had arranged to send them at his own expense, and they had the ear of Cardinal Richelieu, chief minister to King Louis XIII.

The Jesuit priests met open hostility from the settlers and traders in Québec, who were worried that they would interfere in the affairs of the colony. The settlers concerns proved to be justified.

In their letters to Richelieu, the Jesuits criticized the current company's opposition to peace, settlements, and missions, and said Champlain had tried in vain to institute more constructive policies.

Then they took on the interpreters. The Récollets had been complaining that these ne'er-do-wells were interfering with their missionary work, but they couldn't do anything about it. The Jesuits, however, could. They had come armed with the authority to send the interpreters back to France, where they could be brought under control and cleansed of the bad habits of independent thinking and loose morality they had acquired in the wilderness.

The interpreters didn't take kindly to this highhanded treatment, especially when they discovered that the Jesuits wanted them to pass on their knowledge of the native languages to the very men who would replace them.

While many sources claim that Brûlé never left Canada, one story has it that the Jesuits did order him to board a ship for France, along with his old friend, the Montagnais interpreter Nicolas Marsolet.

Marsolet supposedly talked his way out of his banishment by promising to teach the Jesuits the Montagnais language, but Brûlé was less co-operative. The priests had done nothing but malign him from the first day they had arrived. He wouldn't have seen any good reason to help them.

As the story goes, he remained stubborn and was all set to leave, but fell ill just before departure time and the ship sailed without him. If his illness was a ruse, it backfired, because he was kept in the care of the Jesuits. Eventually they wore him down and persuaded him to teach them to speak the language of the Huron.

The final slap in the face came when both interpreters were rewarded for their services by being forced onto the next vessel to France as soon as they were no longer needed.

If this version of events is true, the young men could well have decided they owed the authorities in New France no further loyalty.

If, however, the truth is that Brûlé stayed in New France and carried on as before, living among the Huron and travelling wherever he chose, he probably spent a good part of his time sparring with the priests.

In either case, he was becoming increasingly alienated from the power brokers running New France.

The Fortune One Hundred

Cardinal Richelieu arbitrarily cancelled the charter of Champlain's trading company, and in April 1627, formed the Company of One Hundred Associates. The investors were 100 wealthy men who would share the seigneurial title to a huge swath of North America, from the Arctic Circle to Spanish Florida, and from Newfoundland to the Great Lakes.

The company could make property grants to anyone who would agree to clear the land and bring in settlers to farm it, and would enjoy a permanent fur-trade monopoly. But the company had to commit to settling 200 men of all trades in New France in 1628, and 4000 men and women by 1643. The settlers would be taken care of for three years, then be expected to become self-sufficient on the land they had been granted. No foreigners or Protestants would be allowed inside the colony. Since missionary work would take precedence over all else, three priests were to be settled in each community.

Champlain was appointed Acting Governor of the Colony.

Champlain Betrayed

War broke out between England and France in 1627, and Gervase Kirke, an English merchant who had lived in France and whose wife was French, decided to take advantage of the situation. He formed a company that obtained a commission from Charles I of England, authorizing it to seize Canada from the French. Kirke's sons sailed up the St. Lawrence, took control of Tadoussac, and sent a note to Champlain, politely asking him to surrender Québec.

Champlain just as politely declined. He and his settlers, numbering only 64, were in dire straits after a bitter winter, but they were expecting the ships with a new load of settlers and supplies to arrive any day.

The commander of the English party, David Kirke, decided not to attack the settlement, possibly bluffed into over-estimating its strength by Champlain's cool refusal. On the way back down the St. Lawrence, however, Kirke intercepted and captured the French ships near Gaspé, dealing a disastrous financial blow to the Company of One Hundred Associates and leaving the colonists at Québec waiting for help that wouldn't come.

The settlers spent the summer preparing for winter as best they could, but didn't get much assistance from the Montagnais, with whom relations had become increasingly edgy over the past few years.

In the spring of 1629, the Kirkes returned and anchored their ships at Tadoussac. The reassembled French convoy finally arrived, only to be met by a surprise attack.

Once more the Kirkes sailed up to Québec and demanded the surrender of the colony.

This time Champlain had no choice but to haul

down the French flag. His people were starving.

When he was taken aboard the English ship as a prisoner, two of the first people he saw were Étienne Brûlé and Nicolas Marsolet. And they were not there under duress.

How they got there is another mystery.

Conflicting Scenarios
The "official" story, meaning Champlain's account, was that the interpreters were traitors, pure and simple. According to him, they had paddled down the river to meet the Kirke ship and piloted it to Québec. When Champlain saw them, he was quivering with rage, and he reported every stinging word he threw at them while they stood silent and shame-faced. "May the good God forgive you," he said to them during his long harangue. "I cannot."

Other reports have the interpreters heading down the river to meet the French fleet and pilot it to Québec, finding the Kirke ships instead, and deciding to throw in their lot with the English. Better that than let the settlers starve, they would have told themselves.

In a different scenario, Brûlé, in exile in France, made his way to England, where he agreed to serve Kirke. What was there to stop him? He did not feel any loyalty to the current regime in Québec.

Whatever the actual circumstances, the fact remains that Étienne Brûlé did go over to the English, consigning himself to Champlain's everlasting contempt and French history's hall of shame.

The irony is that by the time Champlain surrendered Québec, England and France had already signed an armistice. As soon as Champlain reached England as Kirke's well-treated prisoner and learned that his settlement had been seized illegally, he began lobbying for its return.

It took a while, but at last, in 1633, Champlain sailed back to his beloved Québec with a new commission from Cardinal Richelieu, and the fleur-de-lis waved proudly over The Habitation once more.

The Jesuit priests, who had had a taste of their own medicine by being sent back to France when the English had taken control of the colony, returned as well.

Murder Most Foul

One final set of mysterious circumstances remains for us to puzzle over in the confusing maze of Étienne Brûlé's shadowy existence.

In the spring of 1633, Étienne Brûlé's life was ended in the Huron village of Touanché, killed by the people he had lived with for 23 years.

Those dry statistics are the only facts of the case.

The theories and speculations surrounding his sudden demise are legion.

He may have been struck down in a crime of passion, executed by order of a tribal council, or assassinated by either a single assailant or a secret cabal.

Tradition has it that Brûlé spent his last years in Huronia sinking into a bottomless pit of despair, a slave to his vices, a man without a country. The French despised him, the English had no further use for him, and the Huron grew tired of his excesses.

Finally, as a result of a quarrel or some sexual indiscretion on his part, or because the Native people realized he had betrayed their beloved Champlain, they turned on him with a vengeance. They tortured and killed him, quartered his body, tossed it into a pot, and devoured his remains in a frenzied cannibal feast.

The inspiration for these lurid stories seems to have been Gabriel Sagard, writing that Brûlé was condemned to death and eaten by the Huron. "The death was perpetrated by the hatred they had for him," Sagard wrote, well after the fact and while he was living in France. "But I don't know what offence he had committed towards them. For several years he had lived in their midst, following the customs of their country and serving as interpreter, and all that he had received in return was a painful death, an abominable and unfortunate ending."

Étienne Brûlé

Father Brébeuf, who was in Huronia in 1634, wrote that Brûlé was murdered, but said nothing about a cannibal feast.

Brébeuf, however, provides us with an important clue to the motive for the killing, a clue he stumbled across several years after the fact.

He and another priest were visiting the Neutral in 1641, at a time when the Huron were concerned about inroads on their trading routes, just as they had been around the time of Brûlé's death. A rumour had spread through the Huron villages that the missionaries were in the Lake Erie region to try to form an alliance with the Seneca against the Huron, using their work among the Neutral as a pretext. The priests received a chilling warning. Be careful, they were told. Another Frenchman had been murdered some years earlier for doing the same thing.

Étienne Brûlé was the only Frenchman who had been killed by the Huron. And he had spent time with both the Neutral and the Seneca.

It is possible Brûlé had been trying to broker a deal between the French and the Seneca. He had promised to do just that when he had escaped torture at the hands of the Seneca in 1615. If he had been able to forge that alliance, he might have found himself back in Champlain's good graces. If the Huron suspected Brûlé was up to something like that, they would have been determined to stop him.

And stop him they did, but at a terrible cost to themselves.

The Huron were nervous of French reprisals when they headed down the St. Lawrence with their furs in the summer of 1633, but Champlain sent a messenger to reassure them that they needn't worry about being punished for Brûlé's death. Étienne Brûlé was no longer considered a Frenchman.

The flotilla went on to Québec, where the customary exchanges of gifts, flowery speeches, and promises reaffirmed the long-standing friendship between the French and the Huron. It was agreed that Father Brébeuf and some of his fellow missionaries would return with the Huron to their homeland. Champlain gave a farewell feast. All seemed well.

But the Huron continued to be haunted by Brûlé's death, their ranks split between those who had committed or condoned the killing and those who had been against it. Some villagers quietly told Father Brébeuf they feared retaliation by the Algonquin and even by members of their own tribe who would take revenge for the interpreter's murder.

In 1634, a smallpox epidemic wiped out half the village of Touanché. Terrified, the people set fire to their longhouses and ran away. As they looked back and saw the smoke curling up to the sky, they swore it took the form of a phantom. The spirit of the sister or some other relative of Brûlé had avenged his death.

They raced to other villages, seeking safety, and took the epidemic with them.

But perhaps it was the spirit of Brûlé himself that brought about the next strange event, one that put Father Brébeuf in a very awkward position.

"He Is Mine"

Every dozen years or so, the Huron held their most important celebration, the Feast of the Dead.

At this festival, the bodies of those who had died since the last festival were removed from the temporary raised tombs in the village cemeteries and buried in a common ossuary.

Usually the feast was held when a large village shifted location, and it would be no longer possible for the living to protect the resting places of their departed loved ones.

Arrangements were made well in advance of the feast, and invitations were sent to the far reaches of Huronia. The feast would last ten days, eight of which were spent preparing the bodies for reburial. This ritual was performed with loving care, regardless of the state of decomposition.

In 1636, one of the chiefs of the Bear Clan went to Father Brébeuf to ask permission to search for the remains of Étienne Brûlé and another Frenchman, who had died of natural causes. He wanted to put the bones of the two men with those of his own family during that year's Feast of the Dead, to symbolize that the French and the Huron had become blood brothers. He also hoped to make amends for the death of Brûlé and pay him a last homage.

Brébeuf found himself in a difficult position. He didn't want Brûlé, a baptized Christian if not a devout one, to be buried as a Huron, but he knew how important the festival was to the Native people.

He proposed to give the Frenchmen a Christian funeral that would take place at the same time as the collective Huron burial, and the bodies of the French would be placed in individual graves near the communal one. He also suggested he would like to erect a large cross on the tomb of the Frenchmen.

Events worked against Brébeuf's plan. A witch doctor told the tribe that a Christian cross was the symbol of a curse. Then a dispute arose over who should organize the feast, the villagers of the relocated Touanché or those of Ossossané. Chief Aenon of Touanché made an impassioned speech, saying he should have Brûlé's remains to bury with his people: "I took him into my canoe at Québec in the shadow of the high rock. His stroke kept time with mine as we paddled up the great rivers and through the white waters. He helped me carry the canoe over long and rough portages. I brought him to the Freshwater Sea and the country of the Hurons. He is mine."

A Huron of Ossossané commented in a rather loud aside that it seemed only right for the Touanché Huron to claim the bones of Brûlé, since they were the ones who had killed him.

It was decided that two separate feasts would be held that year, one in Touanché and one in Ossossané.

It was also decided that the bones of Étienne Brûlé would be left where they were, which was a relief to Father Brébeuf. He hadn't relished the thought of giving that "infamous wretch" the honour of a Christian burial.

So the interpreter remained in the abandoned village of Touanché, and undoubtedly is still there.

And since the precise location of that village is still unknown, even in death Étienne Brûlé remains a man of mystery.

Epilogue

Samuel de Champlain

Champlain died in his beloved Québec in 1635 on Christmas Day at the age of 68. He had collapsed from a stroke in October. The colony still numbered no more than 200 settlers, but it was to endure and become one of North America's most beautiful cities.

The Father of New France would be proud of his only child.

Jean de Brébeuf

In August of 1634, just over a year after Brûlé's death, when Jean de Brébeuf returned to Huronia from Québec, he and his native companions beached their canoe on the shore near Touanché.

The native men refused to go with him to the village, saying it was haunted. He went alone and discovered that the community was just "a fine field … with only one cabin and the ruins of the others."

"I saw the spot where poor Étienne Brûlé was barbarously and treacherously murdered," he wrote to his superior, "which made me think that perhaps some day they might treat me in the same manner."

Epilogue

His premonition was only half-correct. In 1649 he was tortured and killed by the Iroquois. Among his tormentors were Huron warriors who, having been taken prisoner by the Iroquois and adopted by them, regarded the priests as sorcerers responsible for the ruin of their homeland.

But they were so impressed by his fortitude that when he was dead they roasted and ate his heart, and drank his blood, in the hope of gaining his courage.

The Huron

Within two short decades of Étienne Brûlé's death, the mighty Huron Confederacy was destroyed.

Epidemics of smallpox and measles swept through their villages, decimating the population. Attacks by the Iroquois League, armed with English and Dutch firearms, completed the destruction.

The few survivors took refuge wherever they could, gradually making their way to new homelands. Some settled just north of what is now the city of Québec, others to parts of the American mid-west. The Wyandot of Oklahoma are descendants of the people of Huronia, or Wendake.

It is believed that the last fluent speaker of the Huron language in Canada died in 1912.

Bibliography

Armstrong, Joe C. W. *Champlain.* Toronto: MacMillan of Canada, A Division of Canada Publishing Corporation 1987

Bial, Raymond *The Huron.* Tarrytown, New York: Benchmark Books, Marshall Cavendish Corporation 2001

Beaudet, Jean-François *Étienne Brûlé.* Montreal: LIDEC Inc. 1993

Brown, George W., ed. *Dictionary of Canadian Biography.* Vol. 1 Toronto: University of Toronto Press 1966

Champlain, Samuel de, translated by Macklem, Michael *Voyages to New France* (for the years 1615 to 1618) Ottawa: Oberon Press 1970 (First published, Paris 1619)

Cranston, J. H. *Immortal Scoundrel.* Toronto: The Ryerson Press, 1949

Bibliography

Dionne, N.E. *Champlain, Founder of Quebec, Father of New France.* Toronto: University of Toronto Press 1963

Hoxie, Frederick E. ed. *Encylopedia of North American Indians.* Boston: Houghton Mifflin 1996

Jenkins, Kathleen *Montreal, Island City of the St. Lawrence.* Garden City, New York: Doubleday & Company, 1966

Lavender, David *Winner Take All.* The American Trails Series Toronto: McGraw-Hill Book Company, New York, 1977

Morrison, Grace *New France.* Glasgow and Toronto: Farandole Editions 2000

Trigger, Bruce G. *The Children of Aataentsic: A History of the Huron People to 1660.* Montreal, Kingston: McGill-Queen's University Press 1987

Trigger, Bruce G. *Natives and Newcomers: Canada's "Heroic Age" Reconsidered.* Montreal, Kingston: McGill-Queen's University Press 1985

Photo Credits

About the Author

Gail Douglas enjoyed a passing acquaintance with Étienne Brûlé during the 10 years she taught school at the elementary level in her hometown of Sault Ste. Marie. But it wasn't until she decided to write a book about this amazing character that she realized how little is really known about him. She hopes that by putting some flesh on his historical bones she has done justice to the memory of this mysterious character.

Gail left teaching to run a family retail business, then fulfilled a lifelong dream by writing for a small newspaper in Sault Ste. Marie, eventually taking over as editor. She now lives in Oakville, Ontario with her husband Tom, also an author in the Amazing Stories series. She has had 14 romance novels published by Bantam/Doubleday/Dell of New York and these have been translated into more than a dozen foreign languages.

OTHER AMAZING STORIES

These titles are available wherever you buy books. If you have trouble finding the book you want, call the Altitude order desk at 1-800-957-6888, e-mail your request to: orderdesk@altitudepublishing.com or visit our Web site at www.amazingstories.ca

All titles retail for $9.95 Cdn or $7.95 US. (Prices subject to change.)

New AMAZING STORIES titles are published every month. If you would like more information, e-mail your name and mailing address to: amazingstories@altitudepublishing.com.